## About Policy Exchange

Policy Exchange is an independent think tank whose mission is to develop and promote new policy ideas which will foster a free society based on strong communities, personal freedom, limited government, national self-confidence and an enterprise culture. Registered charity no:1096300.

Policy Exchange is committed to an evidence-based approach to policy development. We work in partnership with academics and other experts and commission major studies involving thorough empirical research of alternative policy outcomes. We believe that the policy experience of other countries offers important lessons for government in the UK. We also believe that government has much to learn from business and the voluntary sector.

## Trustees



## About Localis

Localis is an independent research organisation which was set up to develop new ideas for local government. It organises seminars and commissions research relating to all aspects of local government.

# Big Bang Localism

## A Rescue Plan for British Democracy

Simon Jenkins

policy exchange

LOCALIS

First published in November 2004 by Policy Exchange Limited

Policy Exchange
Clutha House
10 Storey's Gate
London SW1P 3AY
Tel: 020 7340 2650
www.policyexchange.org.uk



ISBN 0-9547527-3-2
Printed by Heron, Dawson and Sawyer, London

# Contents

# Preface

This pamphlet arose from a study I conducted in 1995 into the further "nationalisation" of Britain's public sector under the governments of Margaret Thatcher and John Major. Tony Blair's Labour party pledged itself to decentralise that concentration of power and re-establish local democracy. This has not happened, indeed the reverse has occurred. This is a proposal to rectify that failure.

I have long been fascinated by the Cinderellas of British politics. In 1995 I chaired the Commission on Local Democracy (CLD), progenitor of elected mayors and the new localist agenda. Recent events have seen an upsurge of interest in the subject. Localist think tanks are proliferating, notably Policy Exchange, publisher of this pamphlet, and the New Local Government Network (NLGN).

While this work is primarily about Tony Blair's Labour government, it is also about all government. It owes its genesis to a passing challenge from the Tory, David Willetts, that someone "has to make localism sing". I want particularly to thank Anna Randle of the NLGN for her help with research and for her work on elected mayors, of which she is an unquestioned impresario. I thank Tony

Travers LSE for his scholarship in local government, his constant and refreshing scepticism of central government and for reading the text. I also pay tribute to instruction from such pundits as former CLD colleague, Gerry Stoker of Manchester, and David Marquand of Oxford, who have laboured long in the localist vineyard. Nicholas Boles and his staff at Policy Exchange have been most encouraging and efficient.

October 2004

# Introduction

On October 1st 1986, the Thatcher government excised a decayed part of the British economy. It swept aside the restrictive practices of the City of London and its finance markets. The clearing banks lost their retail monopoly. Stockbrokers and jobbers lost their exclusive rights to deal in shares and bonds on the London exchange. The Accepting Houses Committee was broken and British merchant banks became vulnerable to foreign takeover.

The impact was sensational. Old-established banking houses collapsed. Jobs-for-life vanished. The Stock Exchange became a computer terminal. A new breed of Integrated Securities House offered all-purpose financial services to individuals and companies. Many people lost money. Others became very rich. A tradition of oligopolistic trading was replaced by a free market, "lightly regulated". On that day in 1986 the presumption ended that money was best managed by a few London insiders. It was opened to new forms of lenders and borrowers, buyers and sellers, Britons and foreigners alike.

The financial Big Bang restored London as the unquestioned capital of European money, fending off challenges from Frankfurt,

Brussels and even New York. Morgan Stanley switched its Continental base from Paris. The Deutsche Bank moved its headquarters to London. A spirit of competition worked through into every sector of the British economy. There were plenty who thought the revolution would spell disaster. Regulation has certainly had to be fine-tuned. But after two decades none would claim that the Big Bang was a mistake. It worked.

I believe a similar Big Bang is needed for British democracy. It is widely acknowledged that power has become over-concentrated in the institutions of central government. The democratic audit periodically conducted by the University of Essex concluded in 2002, "In the 20th century the UK became one of the most centralised political systems in the western world.... it is hardly surprising that formal citizen participation as voters and as candidates for election has continued to decline."[1]

Britons have noted this and do not like it. Between 1973 and today public opinion has shifted from a belief that on the whole British government works well to a belief that it needs improving, the latter figure rising from 14 to 24 per cent. With this has come a steep rise in public discontent at the quality of welfare services. A YouGov poll in June 2003 showed a majority of British citizens maintaining that "public services have deteriorated under Labour", while MORI recorded a 10 per cent fall in confidence in the government's ability to deliver services locally. Satisfaction with health care is now the lowest in Western Europe.[2]

This pamphlet is about turning back the centralist tide. It is about localism. Much of this involves local government but not that alone. Restoring autonomy to people and institutions involves a wider commitment than just to local democracy, though it can only begin with such democracy. Most people want self-government. Within their families, they wish to be monarchs. Within their communities, they are "communitarians". Beyond the parochial boundary they put their trust in voting, in representative democracy. That requires faith in structures and in other people. Such faith will always be vulnerable to a loss of trust in superior tiers of government, which is why elections are held. Most surveys show British people overwhelmingly in favour of more democracy when asked.[3] One of America's founding fathers, James Adams, declared simply, "Where annual election ends, there slavery begins."

British localism has asserted itself against a central power since the dawn of history. The shires, cities and especially the City of London were treated by the medieval monarch as sources of support and revenue. Shire counties were the pivotal units of local government since before the Norman conquest. Ruled by landowners and gentry, by sheriffs, justices and assize judges, they offered relatively stable and pluralistic rule.

With the dismantling of monastic power under the Tudors, parishes emerged as more or less self-governing entities. Like the urban corporations and boroughs, the parish vestries enjoyed an independence that impressed foreign visitors such as Montesquieu and later de Tocqueville. Cities were granted trading, licensing and taxing powers. Citizens were expected to attend vestry meetings and serve their communities as officials, wardens and jurymen.

When these bodies gave way in the 19th century to a wider franchise, they lost nothing in localist vigour. Elected boroughs and counties levied taxes and dispensed welfare. They relieved the poor and imposed obligations of leadership on the rich (see chapter seven). Macaulay and other historians attributed Britain's long aversion to revolutionary upheaval to precisely such pluralism. It was a spirit which the historian, Tristram Hunt, describes as standing "at the forefront of 19th-century civic culture... channelled so energetically into building the new Jerusalem".[4] It was challenged by Victorian enthusiasm for "national" social reform, but survived in essence until the Second World War.

The decline of localism over the past half century is customarily linked to economic mobility and the decay of once stable social institutions. Prosperity has certainly diminished the extent to which people are stirred to political action. They no longer rise in mass rebellion against the powers that be. Yet there is little evidence of a decline in other forms of "social collectivism". The widely-noted scepticism towards formal politics has not been accompanied by a decline in other forms of collective activity. The British undertake as much voluntary and charitable service as do citizens on the Continent.[5] They are as willing to fight a motorway or a wind farm, what is termed "here-and-now" politics. These are trends, as we shall see, that exist in most Western states.

Two things set Britain apart. The first is the steepness in the decline of its local democracy. The second is that everywhere but in Britain such decline is regarded as needing urgent correction. This is not just because local democracy is part and parcel of democracy itself but because localism is how public services are made accountable to their users. As a result, Britain lags far behind the rest of Europe both in local political morale and in consumer satisfaction in public services.

By way of illustration I give here some stark facts. The following table shows how far British democracy is exceptional in two respects, units of government and number of electors per elected official.[6]

**No. of units of local administration and average population of lowest executive tier:**

| | | |
|---|---|---|
| France: | 36,880 | 1,580 |
| Germany: | 16,514 | 4,925 |
| Spain: | 8,149 | 4,930 |
| Italy: | 8,215 | 7,130 |
| USA: | 35,958 | 7,000 |
| United Kingdom: | 472 | 118,400 |

**Electors per elected official:**

| | |
|---|---|
| France: | 116:1 |
| Germany: | 250:1 |
| Italy: | 397:1 |
| Spain: | 597:1 |
| Sweden: | 667:1 |
| Denmark: | 1,084:1 |
| UK: | 2,605:1 |

Other indicators of democratic health reflect this disparity. A total of 22,745 people serve on local councils in Britain, between a tenth and a twentieth of the number in comparable countries elsewhere. This means that relatively few Britons know, or even know the name of, the person for whom they are voting. (Over 100,000 people sit on parish and community councils but have no executive power, unlike communes abroad.) As a result, average turnout in British local elections has fallen steadily over the past quarter century. It is 80 per cent in Sweden, 70 per cent in Germany and 60 per cent in France. In Britain it is 35 per cent. British general and European elections are no better, recording lower turnouts than anywhere in Western Europe and comparable only with former Communist states.

Meanwhile Britain's local councillors are outnumbered three-to-one by 60,000 unelected people serving on roughly 5,200 local quangos. To them are ascribed functions that may be local but are no longer under local democracy, such as the health service, housing, prisons, training and economic development. There are a further 35,000 unelected magistrates, 345,000 school governors and 30,500 members of centrally appointed quangos. Government patronage – exclusively from the centre – dwarfs the elected sector. The impact of this evolution is specific. While elected councillors divide their time 17 hours with the public to 8 hours with officials, quango members do the opposite, 4 hours with the public to 11 hours with officials.[7] This is the extent of Britain's "democratic deficit".

I am not starry-eyed about localism abroad, though much of this pamphlet draws on its experience. All public administration can be bureaucratic, dilatory, inefficient and corrupt. Local democracy is rarely streamlined and is always easy for outsiders to ridicule. Don Camillos and Don Corleones are everywhere. The exemplar of local subsidiarity, the United States of America, can demonstrate the worst as well as the best local administration anywhere. Nor is the tension between the centre and locality ever resolved. All nations show power being magnetised towards capital cities and power-hungry leaders. The same applies to supranational organisations such as the European Union.

I start with how localism fares in other nations in Europe and America. I do so because such comparison makes Britain's experience particularly vivid. It shows what can and has been achieved elsewhere. I look at recent moves towards decentralism in France, Germany, Italy, Spain, Sweden, Denmark and North America. This is followed by an examination of the opposite trend in Britain, the two great thrusts towards "nationalisation", first under the post-war Attlee government and then since Margaret Thatcher adopted a fierce centralism in the mid-1980s.

Chapter three looks at the apotheosis of centralism under Tony Blair. In Opposition Mr Blair pledged to make local rule "less constrained by central government and more accountable to local people". He would "end Tory rate-capping" and restore business rates to local authorities. He was to be a "communitarian". Apart from the exceptions of Scottish and Welsh devolution, this promise was not fulfilled. The centralist drift continued, notably in education, the police and planning, and was strengthened in health and transport. Regional executive government was left unaccountable and the counties were threatened with abolition.

After Mr Blair's second victory in 2001, the main agencies of centralism, the Treasury, Cabinet Office and Audit Commission, went near berserk. Public administration was overwhelmed with targetry and inspection. Consultants devised ever more fantastic schemes to fast-track, ring-fence and "silo" policy. One official described Downing Street as like Earl Haig's headquarters in the Great War, mechanically shovelling tens of thousands of inspectors over the top to gain six yards of improved service delivery. The period was one of "chaotic centralism".[8]

Many people in Whitehall and Westminster have come to realise that something was going wrong. The system was developing rhetorical antibodies, generically entitled the New Localism. Localism think tanks sprang into life. An education minister, David Miliband, humorously set himself a target-reduction target. The health department began a "cull" of half its quangos and its ministerial boss, John Reid, wrote an ironic pamphlet on "localism in health care". The Treasury claimed no longer to need 80,000 recently acquired civil servants and proposed to cut them. The Audit Commission said it would end "400 targets" and award favoured councils something called "earned autonomy". At the time of writing, these supposed initiatives had yet to yield any results.

Meanwhile the Tories in Opposition under William Hague, Iain Duncan Smith and Michael Howard turned their coats and declared themselves against centralism after all. They were suddenly for local discretion. One Tory ideologue, David Willetts, cited Karl Mannheim that localism was "one of the most distinctive features of Conservatism".[9] The Conservative Policy Unit produced a pamphlet humorously claiming that centralism – "Labour's Command State" – came into existence precisely in 1997 when the Tories lost power. It had led to a "vicious circle of escalating control... and a deluge of political interference in the operation of front-line services."[10] Both parties were showing political cynicism of a high order.

In chapter four I examine the areas in which the Labour government did contrive to devolve some power, to the regions of Scotland, Wales, Northern Ireland and metropolitan London. I also examine the largely abortive attempts of the deputy prime minister, John Prescott, to make his administrative regions more accountable. In chapter five I begin to pull these strands together. What is it we need of a central administration that cannot be achieved locally? What is essential to a state? This leads in chapter six to the nub of localism, money, the fair allocation of national resources and the extent to which redistribution can be "fund-and-forget". How do other countries redistribute resources equitably without Britain's degree of central oversight?

Chapter seven presents the localist programme. Services should be run at the lowest tier commensurate with their efficient and accountable delivery. The message from abroad is that this tier must be realistically "participatory", reflecting local identity and local loyalty. This may imply a regional authority where regions have identity, as in Wales and Scotland. Where they do not, as in most of England, the upper tier is that of a big city or county. Below that tier personal services should be administered at the level of the urban community, municipality and parish. There need be no argument. This is what works.

In chapter eight I argue that such reform in Britain cannot be gradual but must be spectacular. Devolution needs to be comprehensive and overwhelming. I return to the parallel of the Big Bang, to a "bonfire of targets", a mass transfer of power from the centre to locality. This should take place alongside a revitalised local democracy through the widespread introduction of mayors, whether directly or indirectly elected. Voting must be linked once more to responsibility, and responsibility to government. Democracy must recover its "bite".

Chapter nine describes "the enemies", the obstacles to such a programme in Britain. These enemies are political, bureaucratic, professional and, above all, metropolitan. They are embodied in the culture of London's political elite. They are expressed in a media fixation with "post-code lotteries" and in London's distaste for the provinces. As with the financial Big Bang, it will take a giant act of political will to shift them.

In conclusion I point out that a localist Big Bang is not constitutionally radical, nor is it the product of some quaint romanticism. Decentralisation is happening across Europe, where it is synonymous with modernisation. It has occurred within the United Kingdom. It is the norm. I end by describing Norway's millennial inquiry into democracy's future, warning that it cannot be regarded as safe for all time. If not kept in good repair, democracy lies vulnerable to a new authoritarianism, a creature of bureaucrats, regulators, lawyers and the media. Nowhere is it more vulnerable than in Britain.

# 1. Damned Foreigners

> "I know what you are driving at. I knew it from the first. Centralization. No. Never with my consent. Not English."
>
> Charles Dickens, *Our Mutual Friend*

The British pride themselves on their ignorance of politics abroad. Across Europe and America, other nations sharing the same democratic values have the same difficulty maintaining them. Yet few British politicians or officials believe that abroad can teach them anything. When I described the Danish system of localised health care to one official he simply replied, "I don't believe you."

Trips are made to study hospitals in Germany, policing in America, drug control in the Netherlands or urban renewal in Barcelona. But such visits are as to a distant planet. Any suggestion that foreign experience might have application in Britain is ridiculed. So is the idea that what is being studied might be the outcome of local rather than central innovation. When the Home Office goes to New York to study neighbourhood policing, it does so unaware that it is seeing the result of local not central initiative – and that such policing was originally pioneered in Liverpool.

Most public services worldwide are delivered by subnational governments, usually with no more than minimum standards set centrally. Everywhere the principle is declared that services delivery should be delegated downwards – including in countries that have conceded that minimum standards be delegated "upwards" to the European Commission. The only area in which national uniformity tends to be accepted is in financial transfers to individuals, such as pensions and social security. In all other respects, localism rules.

This localism is supported in declarations from the European Union, the Council of Europe, the IMF and the United Nations. For years Britain refused to sign the European Charter for Local Self-Government. This embraces such principles as fiscal discretion, a variety of local tax resources and no ring-fencing of central grants. Article 4 stipulates that local powers shall be "full and exclusive and not undermined or limited by a national or regional authority". No British government could sign such a document with a clear conscience. In 1997 the Labour government duly signed it and continued to ignore it. The charter is unenforceable at present under European law.

## France

Local government in France has often been cited by British observers as the epitome of centralism. The role of the state and its tradition of national assimilation derived from monarchical absolutism, but was reinforced by the absolutism of the Revolutionary 'directoire'. Throughout the 19th and 20th centuries Britons smugly congratulated themselves on avoiding such autocracy through having strong municipal institutions.[11] Since the election of a Socialist president, Francois Mitterrand, in 1982 this has no longer been the case. While France retains large areas of central dirigisme, it has one of the fastest developing devolved administrations in Europe.

At its core is the Republican commune, led by an elected mayor and council, installed in the *mairie* prominent in even the smallest hamlet. The mayor represents the commune in all dealings with the state and runs a variety of local services. His council varies in size from 9 to 69. Until 1982, the mayor and council were subject to a central government *prefet* in every *departement* who needed only to consult them on important decisions. The *departements* date back to the Revolution, created specifically to crush provincial autonomy and possible rebellion. Now numbering 99 they fragmented and straddled boundaries of old provinces such as Brittany and Savoy and were mostly named after rivers, to avoid any hint of civic loyalty: hence Loire, Tarn, Lot and Garonne. The *prefet* was not allowed to come from his own area.

This former relationship between mayors and *prefets* was not uncreative. French cities, like British ones, were centres of welfare innovation. Elected mayors, often with strong local loyalty, restricted the centralist drift. The *cumul* system, whereby mayors were also MPs or even ministers, guarded civic status and promoted local development. Cities such as Nice, Bordeaux and Toulouse prospered mightily under such patronage. But the growth of the welfare state in the 1960s and 70s meant that regulation "slowly imprisoned local government in what was to become a restrictive set of norms."[12]

The defeat of the Gaullists and advent of socialist government in 1981 brought to a head what was strong anti-Paris pressure in the provinces. This was led by socialist mayors and a rising local bureaucracy and middle class, long disempowered by the *prefet* system. New regional bodies created in 1955 as a planning framework became elected authorities with executive chairmen. Their democratic status immediately took root since they corresponded to France's traditional provinces, such as Brittany, Normandy and the Languedoc. Their functions now cover planning, economic development and the provision of *lycees* (secondary schools).

The 1982 'loi Deferre', named after the Socialist mayor of Marseilles, also granted statutory authority to councils at all levels, regional, departmental and communal. This curbed the *prefets* and released local initiative. The *departements* are responsible for local health and social services, roads and further education, but the *prefets* no longer take decisions, merely countersigning those of regional and departmental chairmen to confirm their legality. Any argument goes to independent adjudication, not central decision. It is said that on hearing the passage of the 1982 law some *prefets* broke down and wept.[13]

Jewels in France's localist crown remain the communes. This concept embraces the 'ville de Paris' and the smallest village. 80 per cent have fewer than 1,000 residents. Yet all vote for a mayor, in cities usually as the head name on a party list. Even in small communes the mayor has executive power over building permits and municipal assets, notably the *mairie*, primary schools and historic buildings. More important, he or she is responsible for local development, environment and civic promotion. Service in local government is thus a forcing house for a national career. The result is stark to any visitor to France, from the boosterism of cities such as Lille and Nimes to the quality of parks and squares in every municipality.

Decentralisation in France can be criticised. It is costly and time-consuming. Paris still fights for pre-eminence. Mayors can seem to enjoy too much power, to be vulnerable to corruption and receive too little scrutiny. That in itself proves the radicalism of the 1982 reform. Finance remains a contested area. Roughly half of French local spending is covered by central grants. Half of local taxes come from protesting businesses, making local government highly geared to economic development. But France has a range of local taxes, on buildings, residents (*taxe d'habitation*) and business premises. They are levelled at each tier of local government, giving distinct accountability and democratic bite.

France takes great pride in the 1982 reform. The political potency of provincial France, urban and rural, is its testimony. It laid the spectre of separatism and the turmoil of 1968 to rest. One observer of modern France contrasts "the vitality of local government and of civic participation at the micro-level" with "the disillusionment felt by many French people towards France's great national institutions... and with the decline in activism in virtually all other areas of public and civic life."[14] In France something has worked.

## Germany

Germany hardly needs to decentralise. Devolution was integral to the nation's history and to the post-war settlement. Its kingdoms and principalities were forged into a nation only under Bismarck and made "unitary" only under Hitler. After 1945 the Allies smashed Hitler's *Führerprinzip*, the centralisation of power in Berlin, and pluralised federalism in a new capital, Bonn. Localism was entrenched in the constitution of 1949. The 16 states or *Länder* were made virtual statelets, constitutionally sovereign and immune to Bonn interference. *Länder* representatives in the Bundesrat exercise virtual vetoes on 60 per cent of federal legislation. As a result, *Länder* politics has a potency rare in Europe – some would say an inertial force. There is a German election somewhere every few months.

The concept of local self-government is embodied in a Basic Law. *Länder* and subsidiary counties and cities enjoy a "general competence" to do whatever their electors decide. The *Länder* run public utilities: electricity, water, gas, roads and public transport. They employ the bulk of German civil servants. They collect all taxes and can decide which taxes to levy and how to collect and redistribute them. Below the tier of the *Länder* are counties and municipalities, forming a similar three-tier structure to that in France. Though the larger cities are "unitary" authorities, they are still subject to the *Länder* governments (except as with Berlin where they are both simultaneously).

Each of the *Land* constitutions tend to be different, apparently based on which ally occupied its sector after the war. North Germany tends towards the council model familiar in Britain, with the leader chosen by the council. In the American south leadership is more often by directly elected mayor. Communist East Germany took over Hitler's centralism. Forced to decentralise in 1993, the Eastern *Länder* opted for Bavaria's direct election, an indication of the greater popularity of this constitutional form.[15]

Germany is essentially a confederal state whose public services are run by its constituent subdivisions. Counties and municipalities administer planning, economic promotion, education and social services. Health care in Germany is based on compulsory insurance whose framework is laid down by the centre but implemented by the *Länder*. Doctors are paid by insurers. Half of local hospitals are private or charitable, half are run by *Länder* or municipalities.

Germany shares with Scandinavia a strongly localist political tradition even where, as at present, there is intense pressure for national service standardisation. Its public sector is administered in layers of democratic accountability, shot through with politics. The autonomy of German cities after the war was a key factor in their swift emergence into prosperity. The relative weakness of the centre was a strength. This balance is now much debated, with pressure to reduce the blocking power of the central Bundesrat. But German local democracy is probably the most vigorous in Europe. It is inconceivable that Germans would vote to revert to a centralist regime.

## Sweden

Sweden has a similar pattern of local government to the two-tier parts of England, with 21 counties/regions and 290 municipalities. Yet the use made of this pattern could hardly be more different. The drift of public administration over the past quarter century, especially since the end of the left's ascendancy in the 1980s, has been anti-centralist. An act of 1977 formally devolved most public services to the counties and municipalities, but the counties are essentially creatures of government, their governors appointed by Stockholm and their councils nominated by the political parties.

The main local democracy is expressed through municipalities, many as small as French communes. They run all schools as well as most social welfare institutions, together with town planning and environmental and leisure services. The counties have responsibility for hospitals and medical services. The centre's responsibility for standards – reflecting the post-war "Swedish model" – is represented by the county governor, who also acts as intermediary between the municipalities and the centre. Municipalities and counties both raise local taxes, principally an income tax, financing 75 per cent of their expenditure. This varies between an upper rate of 27 per cent and 33 per cent. On top of national income tax this once helped make Sweden one of the most highly taxed states in Europe.

In 1984 Sweden adopted the "free commune" experiment then spreading across Scandinavia. As David Marquand has observed, this followed "growing evidence during the 1970s of public disillusionment with the public sector, which was seen as unresponsive and over-bureaucratic. Services were not close to the public and failed to involve the public as citizens".[16] The intention of the free commune was to cut overheads, simplify bureaucracy and bring service delivery closer to the public.

Under the first experiment nine municipalities and three counties won almost total autonomy, subject to an audit of fair redistribution between rich and poor. Councils put forward proposals stipulating the areas over which they wanted to take control. Within five years, 284 "freedoms" had been requested, a quarter for schools and the rest involving inspection, regulation, housing, planning and health. Some 20 per cent of requests were rejected by central adjudicators. A number of municipalities requested primary health care from the counties. In 1992 municipalities were empowered to demand further powers, for instance in health services, from the superior counties.

In 1991 Sweden's high-tax system began to crack, largely under the pressure of evasion. This led to the "tax reform of the century". High marginal tax rates were abolished and all but the richest 15 per cent of taxpayers were relieved of central income tax altogether, the burden of welfare finance passing to local authorities. The local income tax was at first capped (as happened in neighbouring Norway), but in 2000 it was uncapped. Poor areas thus got less in revenue than rich ones, but this was compensated by redistributive central block grants. These block grants ended some 100 specific grants existing before 1992.

A result of the reform has been a widespread acceptance of modestly diverging service standards, a clear break with the traditional "Swedish model". One commentator discerned among Swedish municipalities "at least five different policy models, from traditional social democracy to Thatcherite neo-liberalism".[17] The free commune movement appears to have led to more local spending on high-profile services, such as education and environment. In the case of the free communes, the centre has been relegated to indicative target-setting and audit. County and civic pride is strong in Sweden and devolution has been able to capitalise on that, greatly contributing "to the country's democratic, economic, social and cultural development".[18]

Decentralisation has not been uncontroversial. Despite the institution of block grants in 1992, complaints that education was "under funded" led to the ring-fencing of an education grant to municipalities in 2000, an echo of similar moves in Britain. As elsewhere there was evidence that pressure from international league tables was having an impact on central governments to "show performance". Yet in Sweden the localist debate is alive. A parliamentary commission in 2004 considered options for a new local tax regime. It recommended no change in the local income tax since it had clearly "encouraged a high interest and participation in local politics by the Swedish electorate."

## Denmark

Sweden's free commune experiment was followed by Denmark (1985) and Norway (1986). In Denmark this had been preceded by a comprehensive restructuring of the Danish state in 1970, when most public services were devolved to localities. The pattern is of counties (14) roughly the same size as in Britain and municipalities (275). Half the latter are of 10,000 people or less, many no bigger than most French communes. The 1970 principle was that priorities for public services should be set by citizens themselves as close as possible to the point of delivery.

The chief responsibility of the counties is for hospitals, consuming roughly half their budgets and prize exhibits of Danish localism. Counties are also charged with primary health care, secondary schools, planning and transport. The (mostly) subordinate municipalities deal with almost everything else, primary schools and care of the elderly, local roads, culture, sport and the administration of social security. Many such authorities are the size of English parishes, with just one school in their area. The transfer of services between authorities – the dread of British reformers – seems to work satisfactorily.

Denmark's health service is one of universal care, with hospitals open to residents and visitors alike. In 1992 the "right to choose" a hospital in another county was introduced and is now exercised by about 5 per cent of patients. Virtually alone in Europe, the Danish health service has not required huge extra injections of tax money in response to public dissatisfaction. The number of beds has fallen steadily and public spending on hospitals has been roughly constant in real terms over two decades. Denmark spends far less on health than most of Europe, some 6 per cent of GNP. This system registers consistently high levels of public acceptance. In a 1997 LSE study 90 per cent of respondents expressed themselves very or fairly satisfied with the health service, against 48 per cent in Britain.[19]

Two thirds of Danish public spending is by local authorities.

Seventy per cent of county revenue is from local income tax, with 22 per cent from central grants and 5 per cent from property taxes on land. The local income tax rate varies between 9 and 11 per cent and is subject to a national formula of equalisation between rich and poor areas. Local authorities are free to offer different levels of service and for this they levy higher taxes. It is often said (by Britons) that Scandinavian income tax systems are easier to make equitable because income disparities are not as great as in Britain. But high levels of immigration into Scandinavia have made this no longer true, nor is it an objection to such a tax in principle.

Denmark's take-up of the free commune concept was patchy, in part because there was little perceived need of it. A popular variant has been the setting up of ad hoc neighbourhood boards within counties for local planning and schools. Decentralisation, as throughout Scandinavia, has led to an acceptance of variable service standards but with it a dramatic rise in local innovation. There is no desire to return to a greater degree of central control.

## Italy

Local government in Italy reflects both a recent and a more distant past. The fall of Mussolini was followed by a dismantling of fascist centralisation. Measures were introduced to meet the aspirations of Italy's historic kingdoms and dukedoms, especially in the North and far South. Special constitutional status was awarded to Sicily, Sardinia and the Alpine north. As in Germany, the 20 new regions reflected those predating the 19th-century unification of Italy.

Regionalism played a large part in liberating Italy's economic development in the 1980s.[20] Regions and their subsidiary provinces and municipalities took over from central government a wide range of local services, including planning, health, education and economic development. This delegation was reinforced by drastic political devolution in the 1990s, stimulated by dissatisfaction with Italy's inert political structure. Local government reform in 1993 gave provinces and cities directly elected presidents and mayors. They were made powerful, to resist the corrupting influence of national parties and of Rome, and were subject only to votes of confidence by their councils. Whether the resulting "technocratic" rule has avoided Italy's endemic corruption is moot.

There remains a strongly centralist tradition in Italy. Only the special regions enjoy formal legislative powers – indeed they are virtually autonomous. Yet local devolution is now real, capitalising on Italian 'campanilismo' or civic pride. This is reflected in the rising contribution during the 1990s of local taxes to local spending, from 2 per cent to 47 per cent for regions and from 15 per cent to 30 per cent for municipalities.[21]

Robert Putnam, in his classic study of Italian politics,[22] wrote of the crucial role played by decentralisation in the decades after the war. The partly democratic structure of the central state found itself "strengthened not weakened when it faced a vigorous civic society". This has been reinforced by the 1990s decentralisation. Though still on probation, there is no reason to doubt that, for all the ailments of Italian public administration, the tradition of campanilismo has been reinvigorated.

## Spain

In Spain the removal of Franco left a similar challenge to that experienced earlier in Italy: how to appease the separatist ambitions of the Catalan, Galician and Basque peoples. The outcome has been extraordinary. A new constitution forming a "state of autonomies" was implemented in 1978, with devolved powers allowed to develop ad hoc within each region. By 1983 this had yielded a diverse, almost chaotic, pattern of devolution. In the three "ethnic" regions, autonomy was largely determined by what local leaders demanded. Then in 1992 the powers already enjoyed by the Catalans and Basques were made available to all. The delegated functions embraced education, health and local policing. Spain is what might be termed an asymmetrically federal state, with internal government inconsistently devolved to semi-autonomous regions.

Below the level of the region, power in the large cities is vested in strong indirectly-elected mayors, and in rural areas in communes. As in Italy and Germany, Spanish localism is built on a widespread desire to use regional and civic institutions to limit the power of central government. This balance of power is crucial to the stability of Spanish politics. Powerful regional leaders have marshalled their representatives in the Madrid parliament to negotiate ever greater autonomy.

One instance of this was a controversial 1997 reform allocating 30 per cent of national income tax revenue to the regions, with no redistributional element. Regions were also awarded the power to vary local taxes by plus or minus 20 per cent of the national average. They can tax gambling, wealth, financial transfers, vehicles, fuel and property. Subsidiary municipalities can tax property, businesses, construction sites and motor vehicles. In the case of the Basques this devolution is extreme. The Basque country levies its own taxes and it is central government that takes a proportion for national requirements, the reverse of the usual pattern.

Spain now challenges Germany as the most determinedly devolutionist government in Europe. It shows what can be achieved when the political will is present. Nor is there any sign of Spanish people wishing to recoil from it. Decentralisation was considered necessary to cement the newly democratic Spanish state. With the possible exception of the Basque country, that has been achieved. All big countries are to a degree federations. Spain has recognised that, and contrived to modernise its public services at the same time.

## USA

Local government in America might seem a phenomenon far distant from the concerns of Europeans. Yet it is more familiar to most Britons than anything on continental Europe. The mayors of New York and Washington, the governors of California and Florida tend to be better known than any of their British equivalents (except the directly-elected mayor of London). Movies and television have made familiar the offices of senator, state congressman, district attorney, sheriff, marshal and transit authority boss. The terminology of county and borough is taken from Britain. The vitality of American democracy regularly pushes its local authorities into the British headlines.

The principle of subsidiarity is enshrined in the American constitution. States' rights are entrenched. The celebrity of "Hizzonor the Mayor" is much-trumpeted. Yet the only generalisation to make about local government in America is that every variant is practised somewhere. The very word, the state, refers to a local authority, and each has its own constitutional structure. Among states there is a wide gulf between strong and weak governors and mayors. This gulf has quaintly been attributed to the degree of popularity of individual British governors under colonial rule. In America, as in Europe, history is important to local constitutions.

States' rights are respected in regulating cross-border commerce and jealously guarded in such matters as policing and domestic law. States can legislate widely diverging statutes, notably in the treatment of drink and drugs and matrimonial law. Conflict between local police and "the feds" is a running theme of crime movies, as well as real life.

Beneath the state are counties, municipalities and school boards, some 83,000 in all. Just as the state is the primary focus of America's sub-national loyalty, so the municipality, however small, is the focus of sub-state loyalty, usually under an intermediate county tier. Louisiana retains French-style parishes. The Puritan tradition of the Town Meeting still rules many New England communities.

Eighty per cent of Americans live in urban or suburban settlements. They regard almost all government as essentially local. A mayor and council is charged with providing fire and police, roads and sanitation, transport and planning. A separate school board may be responsible for schools. These bodies may levy a variety of local taxes, as may the state. In California taxes can be fixed by local plebiscite, an extension of democracy close to mob rule. The city of New York claims seven local taxes, including income tax, property tax, sales tax, hotel tax and business tax. A flat in New York can bear five times the tax of an equivalent property in London. Texas, in contrast, has no state taxes while cities depend on property taxes, which in turn are far higher than is common in Britain. A suburban villa in Dallas can pay $30,000 a year in local tax.

The system is riddled with tension. But as de Tocqueville famously noted, Americans are proud of their frenetic democracy even as they are contemptuous of its products. Europeans love to point out the low turnouts in American elections. These are heavily affected by America's exceptionally high population mobility and relatively dilatory registration system, which undoubtedly is biased against the migratory populations of inner cities. Turnouts in the suburbs and of "registered" voters beat British levels.

Above all Americans believe in the township. The growth of the new cities of the sunbelt, like the renaissance of the old cities of the rustbelt, has been civic-led. When British ministers and officials go to study "American experience" they are studying local, rarely central, government. It is local innovation that draws them across the Atlantic.

## Conclusion

Various attempts have been made to classify systems of local democracy. Northern Europe deploys localism primarily as a means to an end, the better delivery of public services in a context of communal pride. Southern Europe treats localism as a way of countering central power and appeasing regional sentiment. Its localism is thus a benign consequence of the "escape" from fascism. Some constitutions employ direct election of mayors and governors, others rely on parliamentary and party-dominated structures. In such respects all are different.

Yet there are common strands. The first is that the centre exerts a magnetism in all modern states, reflecting the historic tension between ruler and ruled, capital and province. This applies in nations as diverse as Norway, Germany, France and Italy. The second is that countering this magnetism is everywhere regarded as essential to the modernisation of public services. Third is the contribution of vigorous local participation to such modernisation, to keeping it accountable and making it efficient. Fourth is the role of such locality in fuelling and refreshing national democracy. It is to Britain's divergence from the rest of Europe in all these respects that I now turn.

# 2. The Rise of the Centre

"All England is a suburb of London,"

Henry James

War centralises and defeat decentralises. Germany and Italy centralised in 1939-45 and decentralised thereafter. Britain centralised but did not decentralise. Victory lent authority to the habits of wartime control, which were duly translated into the welfare reforms of the post-war Attlee government. "Nationalisation" was popularly seen as the opposite of private ownership. It was also the opposite of localism. So-called municipal reform had been the engine of civic progress in the century before 1939. It found expression in the civic pride of the great northern cities and in the foundation of the London County Council in 1899.

At the start of the 20th century British public services were administered locally, as they were, and still are, almost everywhere abroad. In 1905 half of all public spending was by local authorities. This embraced schools, clinics, the relief of the poor, asylums and hostels. Local councils ran police forces, technical colleges, public transport, roads, water, gas and electricity. By the Second World War they administered pensions and national assistance and operated a rudimentary structure of town and country planning.

Labour's election victory of 1945 impelled forward the nationalisation of this system. Prisons had been nationalised in 1877. London Transport was nationalised in 1933. After the war, national assistance (social security), public utilities and the railways followed. The New Towns Act of 1946 gave the task of building "the new Britain" not to old cities or counties but to Whitehall corporations. Even public housing, though managed by local councils, was seen as an obligation of central government, which duly paid for it. When fashioning his National Health Service after 1945 Nye Bevan fought against the desire of his colleague, Herbert Morrison, to keep health a local government responsibility. Bevan won, it was said, in part because of his personal dislike for Morrison. He demanded that every hospital manager be "the agent of my department", though it took some 40 years for this to become the case.

Yet the 1945 government still left in place a substantial tier of local democracy. Elected councils governed counties and subordinate urban and rural districts. So-called county boroughs ruled cities of more than 150,000 inhabitants as unitary authorities. These bodies controlled schools and clinics, social services, local transport, water, planning and development. They levied their own property taxes and received central grants, formed into a "block grant" in 1958. An annual "settlement" between Whitehall and local authority associations agreed the overall level of local spending on the rough understanding that it should not rise excessively.

This arrangement survived to the mid-1970s. It was then hit by soaring inflation and the leftward lurch of some high-profile city councils, created by Britain's decayed, essentially cabalistic, structure of local politics. Local government became identified, unfairly overall, with profligacy. It was also associated with the worst era of urban renewal and high-rise housing. In 1975 the Labour environment secretary, Tony Crosland, told local government that "the party's over". A year later, the government suffered a financial crisis of its own making and a savage era of local spending cuts began. Left-wing authorities fought against "the cuts" and duly became the villains of the piece.

The 1980s were a decade of ceaseless war between the centre and locality, which the centre always won. The war was mostly phoney. A measure of central restraint was accepted by almost all local authorities. In the ten years after 1975, local spending remained constant in real terms.[23] At the end of Margaret Thatcher's term it was actually smaller as a percentage of public spending than it was at the start, a fact she resolutely refused to believe. Yet by then all local councils were given standard spending targets. Rates were selectively capped from 1984, a drastic move admitted by officials at the time as "the abolition of local democracy".[24] Then, with a post-Falklands Mrs Thatcher looking for a fight, local government entered her sights with a vengeance. She decided to abolish the rates and introduced instead the West's only poll tax. It contributed to her downfall. What was left of devolved fiscal discretion in Britain fell with her.

The poll tax illustrated the degree to which Westminster felt entitled to adjust the British constitution to its short-term ends. No deference was shown towards any tradition of local autonomy. The tax was claimed to increase local accountability but was promptly capped by the Treasury. It was then surrounded with exclusions, safety nets, rebates and subsidies, all designed to make its introduction politically pain-free, but all reducing its democratic "bite". The poll tax was in truth a covert nationalisation of local finance. Local taxes became merely another way in which the centre raised money for what it regarded as national public services.

By the time of the poll tax's replacement by a banded property tax in 1993, the proportion of local spending covered by local revenue had shrunk from 55 per cent in the mid-eighties to just 20 per cent, of which a tiny fraction was within the discretion of local councils.[25] Four years of upheaval in local taxation had cost the Exchequer some £20 billion in local revenue foregone and shifted to the Exchequer. It was probably the greatest fiasco in the entire history of British public finance.

Most significant was the seizure by the Treasury of business property rates, which had comprised more than half the revenue of local authorities overall. The tax was still levied but fixed at the rate of inflation and remitted straight to the Treasury. It was then folded into the generality of central grants. This deprived local government of a source of locally determined revenue that responded to economic growth and that was available to virtually every local authority across Europe. It destroyed the relationship between councils and their business community. At the time of the transfer in 1990, business rates raised £12 billion for local government against £9 billion from domestic council taxes. This was the biggest act of nationalisation (in cash value) of all time, ironically conducted by a Thatcherite government.

The Tories' nationalisation of so large an area of the public sector began a process that has continued ever since. It converted Britain from what Loughlin and Martin term the "choice" model of local government to the "principal/agent" model.[26] Every facet of public administration became a concern to Parliament. Ministers began answering for every delayed hospital operation, every school budget, every welfare fraud. They took the blame for every library closure, every rent increase and every child care scandal. They demanded credit for every good exam result and every fall in crime, and received criticism for every failure. The most lethal thing they nationalised was blame.

The morale of local government plummeted. Talking to local officials at the time I recall many who commented that their chief foe was no longer lack of resources but "Whitehall interference". In addition, their most interesting and enterprising work, the promotion of economic development, was removed from their discretion. The establishment of well-funded Urban Development Corporations in some big cities cut the ground from under city leadership. Their Tory progenitor, Michael Heseltine, was blunt. Elected bodies, he said, "look too much to the past and too exclusively to the aspirations of the existing population... We took their powers away from them because they were making such a mess of it."[27] The new UDCs would be "free of the inevitable delays of the democratic process". Lenin might have said the same.

I visited Newcastle at this time to plead for help in a project to repaint the five bridges over the Tyne. The capped local council said it had not a penny to spend on such marginal benefits. I should try the local UDC down the road; it was the fount of discretionary resources for Tyneside. This turned out to be true. The bridges were repainted. Similar tales could be told of Manchester, Liverpool, Leeds, Bristol and London's Docklands. The grants and tax breaks awarded to London's UDC were beyond the dreams of elected local government. Infrastructure subsidies and tax breaks to the much-vaunted Canary

Wharf development on the Isle of Dogs made it the most highly subsidised urban renewal project, probably in all Europe.

Enterprise Zones and Urban Development Corporations were Attlee's New Towns reborn. They were little more than conduits for central subsidy, deflecting public investment to where businesses rather than local councils wanted it. This was away from city centres to green field sites on the periphery. It saw a boom in ringroads, warehouse estates, hypermarkets and housing sprawl, the defining emblems of the British landscape in the 1980s and 1990s.

Local government in Britain over this period was treated as if it were part of a colonial empire. Ministers knew they could not administer it directly and so appointed people to run it on whom they knew they could rely. By 1997 there were some 60,000 of these appointees, variously known as the quangocracy or new magistracy. It is now the dominant force in sub-national government in Britain. All were required by Downing Street to be in some sense "one of us".

This was the second of the great culls of British local democracy in the 20th century. It can be best illustrated in the case of London. In 1900 12,000 citizens were elected to help run public services through various councils and single-purpose boards.[28] Attlee's transfer of health, social security and public utilities to the centre halved this number. Lady Thatcher and John Major halved it again, so that in 1997 Londoners voted for just 2,000 elected officials. Yet the seats were not left unfilled. In their place were some 10,000 individuals appointed by central government to new boards and quangos. By the end of the century centralism outnumbered localism in London by five to one.

In 1984 there appeared a white paper with the ominous title of "Streamlining the Cities". It proposed the abolition of the metropolitan county councils established in 1974 for London and the great city regions of Bristol, the Midlands and the North. Most were replaced by their old city corporations, with separate suburban authorities. But London's council, then under the leftwing control of Ken Livingstone's Labour group, was not replaced. The capital became the only metropolis anywhere with no elected city-wide government. It was run, as once had been the American capital of Washington, direct from Parliament. Its rulers were ministers, quangos, joint boards and the gloomily-named London Residuary Body.

Cities and towns elsewhere were hardly better treated. Capped and cramped, civic government was stripped of pride and purpose. The future development of urban Britain was to be anonymous and mechanical, steered by cosy agencies and partnerships such as Business in the Community, Inner City Enterprise, Urban Task Force, City Action, Urban Programme, City Challenge, City Pride and Urban Programme Management Initiative.

Mrs Thatcher justified her centralism on the grounds that she won general elections and could do what she liked. She regarded herself as a true plebiscitary dictator. Her minister, Norman Tebbit, said at the time that the GLC had to go because it was "leftwing, high-spending and at odds with the government's view of the world". The centralist Chancellor, Nigel Lawson, wrote that "so long as public services exist, Treasury control is essential. The alternative is no financial discipline at all".[29]

This was both absurd and hypocritical. The growth of spending under direct Treasury control far outstripped local spending during the Thatcher years. Nor could Lawson's principle cite a shred of evidence from abroad. These were years when city governments in

France, Germany, Spain and Italy were generating an economic renaissance while British cities languished. Directly elected leaders from Barcelona to Baltimore were discovering sources of enterprise that eluded Britain's quangos. Nor did the Tories' centralist institutions pass the test of time or yield public satisfaction. The NHS, British Rail, the schools, universities, police and courts were to endure a quarter century of churning and change, which continues to this day.

Chief beneficiary of this churning was what Michael Power termed the "audit explosion".[30] Its earliest manifestation was league tables for almost all public services. The criteria were opaque and constantly changing (see chapter three). Whatever was quantifiable was important, and what was not was not. The motto was "what can be counted counts". The effect was to increase the nationwide expectation of public service standardisation.

This was manna from Heaven to a range of professions which, in pay and status, swiftly supplanted traditional service deliverers, such as teachers, doctors, social workers and police officers. They were professions which, in essence, told people what to do and saw that it was done. They included managers, accountants, bankers, lawyers and consultants. It was a shift in leadership, as Power commented, "from professions that the public claims to trust more, towards those it claims to trust less". It was a shift from professional discretion and independent judgment towards the culture of obedience – obedience to a London-based norm.

The local government Audit Commission, once an independent accounting agency, increased in size sixfold over the last ten years of the 20th century and came far more under government control. Its first Performance Indicators were introduced in 1992. By 1995 it was producing detailed league tables for a wide variety of council and NHS activities. These included "nights of respite care per 1,000 adults", "percentage of statements on special needs children prepared in six months", "percentage of household waste recycled" and "items issued per head by libraries". The Audit Commission's annual league tables were even sponsored by the accountancy firm, KPMG. It knew what it was about. Such firms were the greatest beneficiaries of the audit explosion.

Auditors could count but they could not deliver. They could encourage or demoralise but they could not create. The Commission for Local Democracy commented in 1995 that "civil servants believe they possess Rolls Royce minds, and local government officers motor-cyclists' minds". But there was no mechanism for getting the Rolls Royces out onto the street if there were no drivers or mechanics. The job advertisements of the Guardian and other public sector journals in the 1990s were heavily biased away from front-line tasks and towards administration and oversight.

The greatest loss was from local politics. The decline in participation through membership of political parties was phenomenal:

| Year | Lab | Con | Lib Dem |
|---|---|---|---|
| 1979 | 666,000 | 1,350,000 | 145,000 |
| 1997 | 405,000 | 400,000 | 100,000 |
| 2001 | 360,000 | 325,000 | 80,000 |

A million Tories simply evaporated. The most serious losses were of suburban and county activists for whom executive power on local councils was a quid pro quo for loyalty at national elections. Visiting a group of Hampshire Tories at the time, I found them bitterly marginalised by the Thatcher and Major governments. They were no longer trusted to fix their rates or spend them responsibly. Thatcher had abandoned a celebrated tenet of her hero, Hayek, that, "Nowhere has democracy worked well without a great measure of local self-government... it provides a school of political training for the people at large as much as for their future leaders."

All over Britain the Tory Party's "little platoons" packed their bags and went home. The Tories were devastated at two elections in a row. Yet they remained determinedly centralist throughout. They opposed Scottish and Welsh devolution. They opposed elected mayors. They protected rate capping and denied local discretion. They did not give an inch. Small wonder urban Britain – and rural Britain beyond the Home Counties – ceased to regard Conservatism as part of its political culture. Contempt for localism cost the Tories dear. By 2004 their best hope was that Labour's equal contempt might drive sentiment back their way. Small wonder they became latter-day converts to the localist cause.

# 3. We Are Really the Masters Now

"We are not the masters now, the people are the masters"

Tony Blair, 1997

On taking office in 1997 Tony Blair respun the heroic cry of post-war Labour. It was a classic Blairism. He carried forward Attlee's "nationalisation" agenda even more vigorously than had Mrs Thatcher and Mr Major, albeit under the rubric of government modernisation. By the end of the century, never in peacetime had any government so completely controlled Britain's public sector machine in all its ramifications.

Any audit of the balance of power between centre and locality under Mr Blair is confused by the generalities and initiatives ceaselessley emanating from Downing Street under his rule. Like his signature of the European Charter of Local Self-Government, what was said was often not meant and what was meant was not said. Daily initiatives became a sort of "virtual government". Media appearance took the place of reality. Public administration often seemed like a Formula One race against the press. A Downing Street announcement of a policy was supposedly enough to implement it.

"Initiativitis", as it came to be called, was a centripetal force, not least within Whitehall itself. A call from the Downing Street press office amounted to a command to "do something" in response to the news of the day, and somehow to prove statistically that it had been done. Since virtually all administration is local in its point of final delivery, the burden this imposed on local officials was greater than ever. In 1999 I sat in the office of a council chief executive and saw on his computer screen some 620 performance indicators to which he was accountable. None were set by his elected council, all emanating ultimately from the Treasury. The number of Whitehall regulatory agencies to which he rendered account had risen in the two years since Labour took office from 57 to 67.

The new Chancellor, Gordon Brown, proved even more centralist than his predecessor, Kenneth Clarke. On taking office he adopted Mr Clarke's overall spending totals but embarked on a long campaign to control more closely what those totals bought. He granted independence to the Bank of England but withdrew it from council leaders. All the battles fought against localism under the Tories were refought under Labour. Even more were won. The phrase "control freak" entered the political lexicon.

The most crucial change was a de facto ending of the old 1958 block grant principle. This had established that central grants to local authorities should be general and not specific. Calculated on the basis of a nationwide assessment of needs and resources, they were for councils to spend as they saw fit. While individual grants might be ring-fenced and the block grant made up of quantities relating to "standard spending assessments", even Mr Clarke respected councils' right to shift resources between services according to circumstance.

Mr Brown's initial control tools were some 600 Public Service Agreements (PSA). Initiated in 1998 these were reached with Whitehall spending departments and tied to planned expenditure. They were a truly Orwellian construct, a computer-based, quantified framework for the entire public sector, to be expanded and refined by individual departments and then imposed on their subordinate agencies and local councils. Onto these PSAs were then spliced 170 "Best Value" indicators for local authorities. These were initially separate from the Audit Commission's previous 1992 performance indicators. The Commission countered Best Value with a further 54 "complementary" indicators of its own. Councils were now expected to perform to two separate sets of targets from Whitehall, causing chaos in town halls.

The targets were entirely top down and applied throughout the public sector. They varied from the specific to the meaningless and embraced the hilarious. Hospitals had targets for vaccination and for cutting deaths from heart disease. Schools had targets for GCSEs, for truants, for class sizes, for reading ages. Academics had targets for scholarly output, with the Treasury at one point measuring the numbers of pages written. Kew Gardens had a target to "receive 30,000 herbarium specimens a year". The Atomic Energy Authority was targeted to "increase the proportion of favourable media coverage by 43.9 per cent". The Meat and Livestock Commission was charged with "maintaining the proportion of people saying they 'eat as much meat as ever'." The Foreign Office had targets for global "peace and stability" and for achieving "a step change in the UK's relations with the rest of Europe". While the idea of an institutional objective was understandable, there seemed no limit to its fatuity in practice.

Whitehall's Best Values indicators were used, among other things, to select "beacon councils", gold stars for conforming to central government norms. The targets left no scope for local variance, diversity being portrayed by the Audit Commission as a sign of failure. There was no question of looking after parks rather than libraries or repairing playing fields rather than schools. As Tony Travers wrote, "No efforts were made to agree the individual targets with those actually running services. When faced with public questioning about how they were set, ministers and officials agreed that many were simply plucked from the air."[31] One official told me at the time, "It is as if a group of chaps in a London club had sat around a table and decided precisely how to govern Britain down to the nearest blade of grass."

There was nothing new in the attempt to quantify units of welfare. The exercise dates back to Bentham, the Webbs and the early socialists. A French observer of 1840s Manchester, Leon Faucher, was shocked to see "everything measured in its results by the standard of utility, and if the beautiful, the great, the noble ever take root in Manchester, they will be developed in accordance with this standard." Dickens was to satirise the same mechanicalism in 'Hard Times', when "every inch of the existence of mankind, from birth to death, was to be a bargain across a counter."

After 1997 such Benthamism became Whitehall's ideology to the point of obsession. The process had begun in the 1980s as services had to be measured for contracting-out purposes. Legal agreements had to be prepared and money attached to delivery. This "re-engineering of government" hugely enriched the new breed of value-for-money auditors in every health, education and social service department, requiring to be matched by an equal and opposite internal audit "echo". Central audit costs duly ballooned, rising in 2001 to a massive £600m.[32] The cost to agencies and councils of complying was probably four times as much.

Nigel Lawson as Chancellor had famously demanded that the Treasury have "a finger in pretty well every pie that the government bakes". By 1999 Mr Blair had four fingers and a thumb. In his conference speech that year he boasted that every local authority in Britain had "500 clear, demanding targets" covering all public services. A year later the office of his deputy, John Prescott, decided the total was 2,500, including 500 for transport alone. The Liberal Democrats claimed the total was more like 6,000. Nor was this targetry just indicative. Hilary Armstrong's Local Government Act 1999 introduced draconian powers to enforce compliance with Best Value targets. Her Clause 14 enabled the centre, by statutory instrument, to vary or overrule anything that a local authority might do, the so-called "Henry VIII" provision. Within two years there were 42 such interventions in local education and social services alone.

The Audit Commission became the Red Guards of what some termed the Treasury's "Cultural Revolution". In the first four years of Labour its costs rose from £80m to £130m, of which its local inspection programme rose from £800,000 to £50m. The result was predictable. Public administration obeyed Goodhart's Law, that any quantified measure of service soon makes the measure the goal. Schools fixed league tables by engineering admissions and exclusions. Hospitals engineered mortality rates by refusing hard cases, and massaged their waiting lists by concentrating on simple operations. The latter in 2003 led the Audit Commission to condemn "major breaches of public trust". But it never blamed its own target culture. Told that crime would be measured by the speed of response to 999 calls, the police increased car speeds and killed hundreds more citizens as a result.

This craze for measurement did no apparent benefit to central government. The Conservative Opposition started measuring the measurements. It claimed in 1998 that only 40 per cent of targets for that year had been met. The government replied that the figure was really 90 per cent. Targets for child poverty, asylum seeking and train punctuality began wandering all over the graph. The education secretary, David Blunkett, pledged himself to resign if his targets were not met, but had changed jobs by the time that proved to be the case. Foreign policy targets came to seem meaningless amid the turmoil of "Blair's wars". In 2004 almost all public transport targets were so unrealistic – such as numbers of people on bicycles and faster train speeds – that they were briskly abandoned.

Targetry was complicated by Mr Brown's other fixation, the "ring-fencing" of central grants attached to particular policy initiatives. These grants exploded in number. For example under the "best safety practice" regime of the "community safety programme", a local council found no fewer than 15 separate organisations were setting it 60 separate targets. Failure to comply with each might jeopardise a funding stream from the Treasury. The London Borough of Hammersmith, seeking to pay for its youth programme, faced 16 funding streams. It opted for those covering Crime and Disorder, Basic Command Units, Building Safer Communities, Domestic Violence Co-ordination, Drugs Strategy Capacity Fund and Criminal Justice Intervention. Each of these streams had, of course, offices and staff in Whitehall, consuming resources before a penny could reach the front line.

The ambition of the Treasury in liaison with Michael Barber and Andrew Adonis, mischievously nicknamed "masters of the Queen's targets" at the new Cabinet Office "Delivery Unit", was to reduce any "heat-loss through executive friction". The jargon held that each pound should be "passported" from the Exchequer down a "policy silo" and out at the point of delivery. The model treated all intermediaries as unnecessary costs, be they Whitehall spending departments or local councils. The Treasury's approach to its subordinates everywhere was like Lord Raglan's at Balaclava, complaining of "young men who knew far too much about war for their own good".

Each public servant was encouraged to see him or herself as the agent of a target. They were told to carry about with them a "mission statement" card covered in banalities about "making the UK a better place for everyone to live in... We want to be the best at everything we do." It did not matter whether the service was locally or nationally accountable, whether it was a school, a hospital, a prison or a care home. Once the centre had declared the policy, the programme and the delivery mechanism, the cheque should pass directly to the point of delivery. It was public administration as minimalist architecture.

One impact of the law of unintended consequences was that councils deprived of discretion over business taxes lost interest in promoting business. This worried the Treasury and gave rise to a typically arcane response. 2003 saw the invention of a Business Growth Incentive Scheme. This promised to direct to particular councils a tiny proportion of any extra rates generated by an increase in its business rate base against the norm, in effect an "incentive to bad planning". The effect was diluted by the triviality of sums raised, rarely more than a few thousand pounds. McLean and McMillan's analysis of "steering centralism"[33] commented wearily, "such ingenuity – to so little purpose".

Another consequence was more serious. The frenzy of target-based executive centralisation overrode the responsibility of professionals. Mr Blair's view that the professions were "agents of conservatism" may in part have been true. But his solution was to repress or by-pass their independence. Professional literature was filled with staff complaining at being deprived of scope for initiative and having to work by the book. Teachers stopped teaching and ticked boxes. Carers stopped caring and watched clocks. Victorian "payment-by-results" for state education had been abandoned by the Edwardians for just this reason.

A survey conducted for the Public Management Foundation in 1999[34] queried the Treasury's belief that civil servants were best motivated by promises of bonuses attached to targets. This bore no relation to how officials saw themselves. In contrast to the private sector, the majority were public servants for a reason, specifically "to improve services to the community". They regarded the public service ethos as real and "recognition for good performance as more important than financial reward". Given that both the centre and locality shared a desire for better services, it was ironic that their view of each other's motives so diverged. As one respondent to the survey said, ministers "just want to use buttons and levers, highly centralist, with more and more performance measurement, no discretion and no local autonomy. It's a shame."

By 2001 senior figures even within Whitehall recognised that some halt had to be called to the prevailing hyperactivity. A white paper appeared that year called "Strong Local Leadership – Quality Public Services". It trumpeted the "magnificent municipal achievements of the 19th century" and called for a rebirth of civic pride, strange in view of the severely centralist regime just introduced under the 1999 Local Government Act. This offered some flexibility to councils over their credit balances. It gave vague promises to reduce central bureaucracy. The sting was in the tail. "Poor performing" councils would receive not the vengeance of their electors but a Whitehall "comprehensive programme of inspections to monitor progress".

Meanwhile more consultants were summoned and task forces appointed to help central direction. In 2004 Mr Brown made the astonishing claim that an adviser, Sir Peter Gershon, had found that 80,000 civil servants, many recently appointed, were not needed after all and could be eliminated or "transferred to the front line". Sir Peter had identified cuts of £9 billion a year in the central government overhead. It was a not-so-tacit admission that centralisation had gone too far and cost too much. Had local government been guilty of such astonishing waste the Treasury's response would have been draconian. It is a curiosity of British practice that the Treasury itself faces no audit and never answers for its public sector management to Parliament. The one thing it happily delegates to subordinate ministers is blame.

Whitehall suddenly declared the new localism as holy writ. The Cabinet Secretary, Sir Andrew Turnbull, announced that "decentralisation hasn't gone far enough" – as if it had gone anywhere – and public services "should work for the man in Whitehall only in so far as they're fulfilling their duty to meet certain minimum standards".[35] The Chancellor's centralist Robespierre, Ed Balls, wrote a pamphlet of breathtaking effrontery. He declared that centralisation "saps morale... destroys innovation and experimentation... and fails to allow that different policy areas must in fact be interconnected".[36] He then went out to centralise the entire English school system.

Whitehall was now awash in double-think. Under a 2002 review of what was quaintly called "devolved decision-making", the number of Public Service Agreements was to be slashed from over 600 to some 130, chiefly by eliminating what were called second-tier service delivery targets. The same pledge was repeated in 2003 and 2004. The Audit Commission also pledged itself to a target cull and the Treasury itself announced a "quango cull". It demanded a halving in the number of Whitehall quangos. They should lose a third of their staff and a quarter of their expenditure. This appeared to be pure spin. Trade and industry staff were simply transferred to Whitehall's fast expanding regional office establishment. A dozen health quangos were eliminated by being merged with each other (see below).

As if eager to parody itself, the new localism led from Best Value to yet another monitoring initiative and another basket of targets, Local Public Service Agreements (LPSAs). Their most novel feature was that they were formed of targets negotiated with Whitehall by local councils themselves. They had the virtue of being voluntary and bottom-up rather than top-down. While LPSAs diluted the purity of Treasury passporting, they at least offered some simplification of what was near inoperable. But they were a third framework of performance targetry for local councils (after Performance Indicators and Best Value).

Nor was this all. LPSAs were in 2002 swamped by yet another initiative from Downing Street, Comprehensive Performance

Assessment. This was a league table of the 150 English county and unitary authorities, measured by the Audit Commission on the basis of a matrix of central and local targets. It was mellowed by subjective judgments by inspectors and by councils' own declaration of priorities. It was promoted as "a framework for increased decentralisation" and yielded a football league structure of five divisions, with 22 "excellent" councils in the top division. These last were allowed to form an "Innovation Forum", to negotiate a range of benefits and freedoms from Whitehall. It was a distant echo of the Scandinavian free commune.

There is no doubt that some within Whitehall saw the CPAs as a genuine effort to reverse the centralist frenzy. The Cabinet Secretary, Sir Andrew Turnbull, wanted a return to block granting, and a number of permanent secretaries realised that targetry and ring-fencing were driving them towards a wholly nationalised public sector and an intolerable burden on them and their ministers. Targetry was now costing hundreds of millions of pounds to administer. But if the CPA principle was to be decentralist it required the centre to restore proper financial discretion among other freedoms.

This did not happen. The Treasury soon let it be known that there was to be no real autonomy. Any council that dropped out of the top division – as judged by the government – would, as one put it, "lose all its air miles". This monumental paternalism was reinforced in 2003 when a number of highly rated councils were ordered to give more money to their schools following front-page headlines over "school budget cuts". This was followed by a law enforcing the passporting of all education funds from Whitehall to schools and the full ring-fencing of central support for education.

No sooner was Comprehensive Performance Assessment up and running than yet another initiative appeared, twenty-one "Local Area Agreements". These sought not to re-establish block grants but simply to compress some 70 revenue streams other than education into just 3 pots (see chapter six). These in effect formalised the end of the 1958 settlement and confirmed local councils as agents of central government. The government declared there would be a return to rate-capping, no reform to council tax or any restoration of business rates. It was little more than a clearing away of some of the undergrowth of the previous few years. And it was merely an experiment. As we have seen, Sweden a decade earlier had cleared away 100 revenue streams in establishing a single local block grant. Yet Britain still had to "experiment".

I examine below the impact of these developments on a range of Britain's public services. I should begin by accepting that most perform adequately. Since the public sector now consumes over 40 per cent of the gross national product, so they should. But all are enveloped in political turbulence and many are felt by the public in some sense to be failing. A poll in June 2003 showed a majority of British citizens thought "public services have deteriorated under Labour".[37] This even applied where, as in hospitals, people often approved of their local institutions. It was the "national" that was at fault.

All of the services I discuss are essentially local in delivery, in the sense that they are personal or communal rather than statist. Some are supposedly under the remit of local democracy, others have already been nationalised. Yet the government's approach to all, be they health, education or public transport, has been equally interventionist. This suggests that the denizens of Westminster and Whitehall are not averse to local democracy as such. Their disregard of localism in all its forms is rooted in a cruder fixation with control. It is a control that seems always to end in tears.

## The schools

In 1997 schools in England and Wales were still mostly owned and run locally, by city and county councils. The new Labour government ended one centralist Tory policy, the grant-aiding of schools that chose to "opt out" of local control. These schools were mostly selective. Opting out enabled them to escape the egalitarian rigours of the comprehensive admissions system. For a while local authorities were left to plan state schools as a whole. It did not last for long.

Labour's first education secretary was also its most interventionist minister, David Blunkett. He immediately went further than the Tories and extended testing regimes in primary and secondary schools, despite the aversion of many in his party to this performance measure. School testing in the 19th century had relied on such quantification, and had been abandoned. Teachers were simply teaching the test, with consequences cruelly satirised in Dickens's 'Hard Times'. Even when Scotland and Wales refused to institute such regimes (see chapter four) the government insisted on them for England.

Mr Blunkett introduced a stream of initiatives to meet each perceived failing in the local education service. In his first two years, he found himself issuing 315 consultation papers, 387 regulations and 437 items of guidance. Hansard reported that, in 2001 alone, schools received 3,840 pages of instructions from London, or 20 pages per school day.[38] These even included a "Bureaucracy-cutting toolkit", which appeared in three volumes. My local primary school found itself having to fill in forms for a Fair Funding formula, a Numeracy Hour, Revised Desirable Learnings Outcomes, Home/School Agreements, New Admissions Strategies and a plethora of returns on bullying and truancy. It had to prepare a pay-linked appraisal scheme and a local development plan. Meanwhile its head, if she had time, could apply for one of 26 grant streams, ranging from drug prevention to building security. Her neighbouring secondary schools could add Social Inclusion money, Excellence in Cities money, National Grid for Learning grants, Behaviour Improvement grants and myriad other streams of cash.

The government then demanded that every child spend 20 minutes each evening hearing a bedtime story. A year later this target was raised to half an hour of homework below the age of 11 and 90 minutes thereafter. Then came a £100 on-the-spot fine and even imprisonment for parents whose children failed to attend school. Eighty-eight per cent of teachers opposed this punishment, which would clearly disrupt relations with parents and pupils.[39] Since schools had a financial incentive to improve their exam results, they also had an incentive to exclude persistent truants. Yet the government, in a blaze of publicity, imprisoned an Oxfordshire mother for the truancy of her daughter, in no way improving the girl's attendance record.

In 2003 came a collapse in relations between London and local authorities following the settlement of the education component in the central grant. The lack of flexibility in the grant formula left councils with little scope to meet an extravagant increase (negotiated by central government) in teacher pay and pensions. Schools found themselves forced to lay-off teachers and abandon extra-curricular work. While extra money had been given by the centre for education, the distribution was not pro rata. Whitehall priorities were banging up against each other and ring-fenced grants were proving inflexible to meet changing local needs. The governors of a Chatham school were pleading with parents for what amounted to voluntary fees, despite having been told by the new education secretary, Charles Clarke, that the government had since 1997 spent "£800 more per pupil in real terms, a 25 per cent increase".

A media blitz over "sacked teachers" induced a desperate government to increase its control. The 2002 Education Act had already empowered Whitehall to intervene to enforce "passporting" of central funds to local school budgets. This involved yet more targetry to ensure the money was properly spent. The Audit Commission concluded that the imbroglio was largely the result of central government funding procedures yet demanded still more financial information from schools. It protested that education attracted "the least amount of scrutiny" in the public sector and called on local councils to engage "more fully in financial management, challenge, support and intervention". Both government and local councils needed a "more solid understanding of schools' budget positions".

Then in summer 2004 a furious argument broke out between the Treasury and the Cabinet Office's Mr Adonis on one side and the education secretary, Charles Clarke, on the other. The issue was Mr Adonis's revival of the old Treasury determination to abolish local education authorities and replace them with a national schools service to parallel the NHS. The outcome was a compromise. The government announced the virtual suspension of local government running of schools. In future school planning and development would pass to the Secretary of State, who duly published a Five-Year Plan. He wanted all "best performing" secondary schools to revert to Tory direct grant status, so recently abolished.

Governors could now choose from a menu of grammar schools, city colleges, academies or specialist schools, with central grants "100 per cent passported". The new semi-privatised academies were revealed to be costing an average of £23m to build, way above local authority costs.[40] A number of "business sponsors" also turned out to be expensive suppliers of goods and labour to institutions they were sponsoring. Local councils would be left dealing with admissions refusals and a residuum of unpopular and "special needs" schools. The government was now a hair's breadth away from the complete nationalisation of Britain's schools. It had casually ended a century of local control of these institutions, and ended both the 1944 Education Act settlement and the 1965 comprehensive reorganisation, on which Labour had fought four decades of elections.

Any thesis that central control would be less bureaucratic than local was denied by schools' Whitehall mailbag. By 2004 institutions which Downing Street wanted to call "independent" and free of local government oppression confronted 350 policy targets and 175 efficiency targets. A junior education minister, David Miliband, even set himself the ironic target of reducing his targets. He wanted a "25 per cent reduction in inspection... a 30 per cent cut in exam red tape... and a 40 per cent cut in data submission". He promised an end to the paper blizzard and something called "simplified funding". I assume he was smiling. At the time of writing, the local accountability of Britain's schools is less probably than anywhere else in the world.

## The police

Policing is among the most local public services. Its purpose is to provide neighbourhood security. It must be "accountable at the point of delivery" or it is not accountable at all. Britain's city and county forces, of which there were 126 in 1968, had always been governed by local Watch Committees and answerable to local representatives. Since the days of Robert Peel, central government wanted its own security force, but since Peel libertarians and socialists alike had resisted any such concept as smacking of an authoritarian state. The suggestion was derided with the French word, 'gendarmerie'. The only force in Britain run directly by the Home Office was London's Metropolitan Police.

The story of the British police in the 1980s and 1990s is of remorseless concentration. Its activities were target-driven and its budgets ring-fenced first under Michael Howard as Home Secretary and then under Jack Straw and David Blunkett. Forces were amalgamated under the Tories, coming down to 43 in England and Wales. In 1988 a matrix of performance indicators was determining police numbers, pay and conditions, service, and investment and equipment. Virtually all major spending required Home Office approval. This was despite the irony that the one force directly run by the Home Office, in London, was on every historic performance measure the least efficient and most costly.[41]

Kenneth Clarke, Home Secretary in 1993, remarked that he had "no faith in putting elected people in a position to run the management... of the police service". He decided that "all police authorities will be independent of local councils", under the command of his own officials. Only a rebellion in the House of Lords stopped his achieving this nationalisation. Another such rebellion stopped his successor, Michael Howard, from yet again halving the number of police forces to 25. In 2004 the Home Office returned to this campaign and mooted the same objective.

There is no shred of evidence that big forces are more accountable or efficient than small ones. Indeed, in a recent Policy Exchange study, Barry Loveday and Anna Reid have shown that big forces with invisible lines of accountability tend to perform worse than small, local ones. This is true not just within Britain but in contrasting forces abroad. The nationalised police of France and the Netherlands tend to be unpopular. The most innovative policing and recently the fastest falls in crime have been in highly localised American cities. Loveday and Reid's conclusions are unequivocal. Central control does not yield more effective policing, but it does yield greater expense.

The 1994 Police Act demanded that just half of authority members be elected councillors. That act, according to its white paper, set out to "refocus police priorities and direct them to those things which the government considers the police should be tackling as priority tasks across the country". This centralisation was passionately opposed by the Labour Opposition at the time. It was described as "the act of a government that resents local freedom with an aversion bordering on paranoia". The speaker of those words was one Tony Blair.[42]

Mr Blair further centralised control of the police in his 2002 Police Reform Act, one of ten reforms to law and order which he produced in just five years of government. The act enabled the Home Secretary to sack chief constables, demand "action plans for failing forces" and "codes of practice" where required. In 2004 Mr Blunkett, moved from education, duly suspended the chief constable of Humberside following a media outcry after the Soham murders the year before. It provoked a full confrontation with the local police authority, which considered its chief constable unfairly victimised.

In London the Metropolitan Police had supposedly been devolved to the new Greater London Authority (see chapter four), yet the Home Secretary continued to behave as if he still ran it. He retained the power to fix the police budget and to vet senior appointments. Sir John Stevens, first commissioner of the reconstituted London force, told me he was accountable to 14 separate points of authority. Between 2001 and 2004 he had to deal with 154 central crime "initiatives", some of staggering triviality. They embraced shopping centre crime, mobile phone crime, credit card fraud, football hooliganism, internet child abuse, anti-social behaviour, crime "hotspots", crack houses and curfews. Not one came from his own police authority, which had its own set of requirements and targets.

Mr Blunkett was now behaving like the nation's policeman-in-chief. His 2002 "Safer Streets" programme targeted selected communities across England with extra police on a ring-fenced central budget. Some temporary reduction in muggings was achieved – and trumpeted nationwide – but the cost was put at £67m, or £14,000 per mugging temporarily prevented. The exercise was purely one of centralist grandstanding for media display.

Ring-fencing was most bizarre in the context of traffic management. The growth in urban road congestion was leading authorities to impose ever higher parking tolls and, in London's case, a computerised congestion charge. Added to speeding fines this became a major source of revenue for local government. In the City of Westminster, parking revenue in 2004 equalled the total received from the domestic rates.

Under ring-fencing, this money could only be devoted to traffic and transport expenditure. The effect was not only to give local authorities an incentive to increase their fine revenue but to find ever more ingenious ways of gathering it – to widely-publicised popular resentment. It also led to lavish spending on road repairs while other local services languished. London roads and pavements seemed almost permanently disrupted, especially towards the end of each budgetary year. Local councils were banned by central government from limiting the freedom of private or public utilities to dig up roads. The resulting chaos – London's Camden High Street was dug up 80 times in one year – was a public demonstration of the impotence of British local government.

In 2003 the Home Office appeared fleetingly to recognise that its reactive initiatives had gone too far. A half of all police time was being spent on administration. It mooted the introduction of elected boards to which local forces might answer, a ghost of the old watch committees. So-called "crime reduction partnerships" would seek to re-establish the link between police command units and parish and town councils. This was in part a response to the biggest growth area in law and order, the recruitment by wealthy neighbourhoods of private security firms to patrol their streets. There are now four "police" organisations in Oxford Street alone, the Met, Westminster's police support officers, the West End partnership's patrol staff and the stores' own security guards.

In most parts of urban Britain an increasingly nationalised police force is seen to have failed at the point of delivery. Though property crime has declined long term, more worrying muggings, street violence and gun crime continue to rise. So does the morass surrounding the drugs industry, where the centre refuses to concede local licensing or Dutch-style regulation. As a result, British communities have come to look elsewhere for protection, paid out of their own resources. The greatest irony of the campaign by both Tory and Labour Home Secretaries to nationalise the police is that it has put Shakespeare's Constable Dogberry back in business.

## Planning

The most serious Labour inroad into local democracy was in perhaps the least expected area. A series of speeches from John Prescott attacking county planning culminated in his 2004 Planning and Compulsory Purchase Act. This stripped counties of any substantive planning role. They had previously determined everything from rural conservation to economic development. These functions would now fall to the regional offices of Mr Prescott's own department. In a fierce debate in the House of Lords, the peers attempted to limit this usurpation to areas with elected regional assemblies, as yet non-existent. The government refused to tolerate this. The only accountability it would concede was to "regional planning boards" appointed by itself (see next chapter). Policy and decision remained with Whitehall.

The planning system had certainly become cumbersome and the act's ambition to expedite it was laudable. But the centralism was total. Regional officials of Whitehall would determine Regional Spatial Strategies, approved by the Treasury. These would embrace development and employment, the conversion of farmland to industrial use, new towns and expanded villages, and the setting of individual district housing targets. All these policies were target-driven, the targets prepared and enforced entirely by government. The allocation of housing totals to counties on the basis of census demography bore no relation to population movement or changes in taxes, prices or second-home demand. It sought to quantify housing "need" on a county basis, when in reality it was simply planning responding to increased demand. Such "predict-and-provide" planning had long been discredited in road building.

In future not even cities the size of Bristol or Nottingham would be allowed to make decisions on their future character or appearance. Local districts and unitary authorities were charged with preparing Local Development Frameworks, but these had to be within the terms and boundaries of the Regional Strategy. Existing settlements, be they towns or hamlets, could no longer protect their surrounding countryside or declare green belts. Central government's powers embraced the enforcement of wind turbines and phone masts in rural areas. A residual power to allow villages to draw up local "landscape maps" was withdrawn in 2004 when a Somerset village had the temerity to use it.

Coupled with the de facto ending of local running of schools, the demise of structure planning stripped the English counties of democratic purpose. The Local Government Association regarded the 2004 Act as the death of the new localism. It called it "the old centralism managed by a regional branch office". The proposed system was widely ridiculed. It was likened to the Luftwaffe (by the Spectator), Soviet social engineering (by The Times) and the death of rural England (by the Green Party). Mr Blair and Mr Prescott were unmoved.

The 2004 Act imposed central targets on the local planning framework to a degree unknown in England and unheard of elsewhere in Europe. It marked the end of popular control over the evolution of the English landscape, control that ran from the Middle Ages through the Industrial Revolution to the end of the 20th century. It was a return to the ancient prerogative of "the king's forests".

Central government was initiating a truly nationalised system of land use of a sort familiar only to communism. The spread of low-density development which had already been witnessed across central and southern Britain since the mid-1980s continued unchecked under Labour. But now the centre ordained that "rural development" was to mean, in effect, urbanisation. The best indicator of this was the response of the market. Within months of the 2004 Act being passed, fields in the once-protected Cotswolds Area of Outstanding Natural Beauty were being sold as building plots. Though none had planning permission, the speculators were gambling that government would override local planning control and turn hundreds of pounds in hundreds of thousands. The certainty that government would protect rural England had been replaced by the likelihood of development. If the Cotswolds was not "safe", where was?

## The National Health Service

Education, the police and planning are local government functions being usurped by central government. The National Health Service is already run by central government, the only such service anywhere in Europe. For decades it has been undeniably popular, a matter of British pride in comparison with systems elsewhere. Those days are over.

The World Health Organisation now puts British health care 17th, behind all comparable countries, in "responsiveness to the needs of patients". A decade of change led, in 1997, to 41 per cent of British consumers expressing dissatisfaction with their health service. The equivalent figures for France and Germany were 15 per cent and 11 per cent respectively. Today over half of Britons want their service changed, while 70-80 per cent of Scandinavians are content with theirs.

Labour in 1997 promised "no return to the top-down management of the 1970s" and a "rooting out of unnecessary administrative costs". It then did the opposite. Some 40 central health service agencies were created, burdening hospitals and GPs with over 400 targets. In 2001 came a 10-year plan, instantly superseded by an upheaval over the setting up of foundation hospital trusts. A new NHS Act in 2002 gave the health secretary 58 further powers he claimed to need to control the service. Millions were now being spent on central agencies such as a National Institute for Clinical Excellence, a Commission for Health Improvement, an NHS Modernisation Agency, a Patients Access Team and a dozen "health tsars". The Institute of Health Care Managers had 1,700 separate job categories in 1995 and 5,529 in 2002. Centralisation had gone berserk.

The Tories had promised in 1989 to free hospitals of central control under "trusts", an independence bitterly opposed by Labour as threatening the internal equity of the NHS. The trusts brought about no change. The NHS hierarchy simply refused to divest itself of central power. An office block of Stalinist proportions was built in Leeds to perform functions supposedly superseded by trust-status. The resulting system was described by a Plymouth surgeon as "like being in Russia under the 5-year Plan". His budget was charged £1,500 for a shelf that cost £100 at a local store. NHS administrators became obsessed with ending "postcode health lotteries". Day surgery as a percentage of all surgery was found to be 73 per cent in Croydon and 56 per cent in Oxford. A baby born in Rutland had a life expectancy of 79.5 years, in Manchester only 71. This was thought unacceptable, or at least an excuse for more control.

Leagues tables of ever greater complexity were constantly challenged by hospitals, who pointed out that such statistics were costly to prepare and easily distorted by devious administrators. Hardly a day passed without an official being disciplined for "fixing" a waiting list, sometimes to benefit his personal bonus. Bureaucracy was rampant. In 1997, hospital medical staff were increasing by 4 per cent a year and administrative staff hardly at all. By 2001, medical staff were rising by 3 per cent and administrative staff by double that.

The government reacted by reviving the Tory trust hospital concept, as they had revived Tory direct grant status for schools. Twenty "foundation" hospitals, winners of three stars in the latest league table, would "earn autonomy", with the boon of an elected "independent public benefit corporation board", with freedom from bureaucracy. These boards were ostensibly an innovation, like American elected School Boards, and were the brainchild of the Cabinet Office. In future, patients, staff and random members of the public would be invited to nominate themselves as an electorate to vote for members of the new hospital boards.

Nothing better displayed the cynicism with which Mr Blair and his colleagues treated the new localism. The foundation boundaries bore no relation to any known area of local identity. The Birmingham Heartlands and Solihull Trust served a million people in the Midlands. The Guy's and Thomas's Trust served half a million people in South London. The 20 hospital trusts contrived by local mailing and advertisements to gather a collective electorate of 240,000 people but these were hopelessly unrepresentative of any community. Guy's and Thomas's mailed 230,000 local households, but just 500 responded. Of the eventual 3,700 votes cast, 39 per cent were staff. No trust attracted even one per cent of its true catchment area as voters.[43]

The clear danger of entryism by trade unions or special interest groups was met by the Department of Health announcing that the boards would have no power. They would not be independent but operate within a framework of standards and quality more or less as before. This was the outcome of a battle between Mr Brown and the then health secretary, Alan Milburn, who afterwards resigned from ministerial office. To rub salt in the wound, Bill Moyes, the "independent foundation hospitals regulator", remarked that if any hospital lost one of its stars it would also lose foundation status and thus autonomy. Its elected structure would collapse and return "to being performance-managed by the Department of Health".

That is the fate that loomed in July 2004 when a new "Healthcare Commission" stripped 4 of the 20 existing trusts of a star and likewise demoted 10 out of 31 new applicants for trust status. The King's Fund issued a report concluding that "stars are a good way of rating hotels but don't work so well for complex organisations like hospitals".[44] It was unfortunate that at the same time the new health secretary, John Reid, joined the localist bandwagon with a pamphlet trumpeting trusts as moving "beyond local managerialism into genuine local ownership".[45] National uniformity of provision, he admitted, "has not delivered equality." Equality remained his goal but hospital devolution was clearly not going to achieve it. Within weeks he was launching yet another initiative of what Downing

Street called "beacon behaviour". He and 11 other "health tsars" spread out across the country and "saturation bombed" local health operations.[46]

The elected trust boards were a stab at democratic decentralisation. They were given no chance of working. A veteran NHS observer, Rudolph Klein, wrote that there was no point in an election that was window dressing. The government was displaying "complete cynicism about the role of the governing boards". Given the political effort that had gone into setting up the trusts, there was "little convincing evidence that these changes have improved quality of care, satisfaction or health outcomes".[47]

In August 2004 The Times reported that the foundation executives had protested to the NHS that none of the promised freedoms had materialised. The head of the Chester Trust vividly commented, "the bureaucracy is swarming round us like antibodies round an infection, trying to kill us off." The hospital regulator, Mr Moyes, admitted that "things seem to be getting worse rather than better".[48] He was sure this was temporary. Hospital foundations had gone the same way as Mrs Thatcher's trusts.

In 2004 the Department of Health made a last effort to curb what was now two decades of administrative frenzy. It announced a "Change Programme" to reorganise 14 NHS "directorates" into 3 "business groups". There was to be a cull of half its quangos and an admission that 25 per cent of their staff and an astonishing £500m of bureaucracy were unnecessary. Bodies with such titles as The Commission for Patient and Public Involvement in Health and the Health Development Agency were to be abolished. A troubled NHS information technology project, costing some £2.3 billion, would soothe the doctors' troubled brows.

When I first studied the NHS ten years ago, I concluded that the turbulent reforms of the Thatcher era had done no more than complete what Bevan began in 1947, achieving the true nationalisation of Britain's health service. But that exercise had led to an uncomfortable consequence. It had eroded the relationship of trust between doctor and patient and between hospital and community. A new and cruder accountability to quantifiable targets had come in their place. The outcome would be a loss of confidence, protective medicine and an explosion of negligence claims.

This has come to pass. Britain's health service is governmentally out of date. Like many high-profile nationalised industries, it has become a politically unstable entity. Public opinion is turbulent. Ministers have no subordinate authorities to which accountability can be passed and therefore cannot leave it alone. In one extraordinary scene in the House of Commons in 2003, the Prime Minister and the Leader of the Opposition wrangled over how long a named patient in a London emergency department had waited to be seen.

While the rest of Europe was mostly satisfied with its (local) health service, Britain's national one was wrestling with a centralisation that had failed. A desparate Labour government is now proposing what was once unmentionable, the extensive privatisation of British health care.

## The railways

Britain's railways in the 1990s were not supposed to be in the public sector. They were entirely owned by private shareholders. That did not stop British governments from regulating them near to death. From 1997 to 2004 the trains moved from regulation to control to partial nationalisation to virtual nationalisation. The sequence was astonishing and, in the words of the 2004 railways white paper, "a failure". But failure on whose part?

In the final years of public ownership in the 1980s, the railway was aiming for financial self-sufficiency. It came close to achieving it. The main inter-city and London suburban services, together with freight and parcels, were either profitable or budgeted to break even. The recession of early 1990s led to these targets being missed but it was reasonable to expect in time that only cross-country and provincial suburban services would require long-term subsidy. Had British Rail planners been told that economic growth would raise demand across Europe by 25 per cent in the 1990s, they would happily have accepted a break-even.

This arm's-length model of a national railway with sub-contracted local services was viable. Local Passenger Transport Authorities were either purchasing services from British Rail or, in the case of Tyneside, running their own trains. Such a service could have been privatised, either as a whole or by reviving the old regional companies. Or it could have been established as a trust, with freedom to borrow in the market against future revenue, as in many cases abroad. No such plan was allowed. The Treasury decided to fragment the railway's management structure on the basis of myriad sub-contracts, each regulated by a superstructure of extraordinary complexity. It was said that the Paddington staff lavatories required 600 pages of contractual agreements.

The impact of fragmentation on a highly time-sensitive service was catastrophic. Within a decade, Britain's railways were a morass of 25 companies with interlocking contracts more intrusively regulated than ever under nationalisation. Costs rose as defensive management permeated every corner of the industry. Restoring a mile of track was reputed to be three times more expensive than under British Rail. The infrastructure company, Railtrack, was eventually abolished and renationalised as Network Rail. Trains began to eat up more than double British Rail's former subsidy. Far from privatisation freeing the railway from central expense and control, it increased them. Public complaints rose sharply.

By 2001, the monitoring of the railway by Whitehall paralleled that of local government. A new Strategic Rail Authority (SRA) ran alongside an Office of Rail Regulation and an expanded Whitehall rail directorate. On my calculation, since privatisation the rail industry "overhead" went from roughly 400 people above the level of oporational management under British Rail to over 4,000. The SRA was setting targets Whitehall-style for what were supposedly private companies that embraced everything from punctuality to lavatory cleaning and litter. By 2004 the train operating companies were little more than state sub-contractors. Their revenue was dominated by their ability to claim subsidies, penalties and internal price transfers.

In 2004 this structure experienced a genuine crisis. The government decided to abolish its own creation, the SRA. Strategic planning would be brought within the transport department under a "directorate of railways". Franchise regulation and performance oversight were assigned to yet another regulator, the Office of Rail Regulation under its own six member board. A nationalised railway that had been restructuring itself in response to local service priorities was brought under the lash of central targetry.

The renationalisation of the railway was a tragedy for everyone, for managers, staff, passengers and the reputation of privatisation. It was certainly a disaster for localism. Most non-intercity train services are local. When the Commission for Integrated Transport asked local council transport managers whether central strategic direction accorded with their own, 68 per cent said no, only 23 per cent said yes. They were agents of policies related to their areas with which they disagreed.

Only one area of the network ran counter to this centralisation. Train services in Scotland and Wales were formally handed, under block grant, to their new devolved executives. For some reason, these parts of the network were different. To that difference I now turn.

# 4. The Great Escapes

> "When any community is subordinately connected with another, the great danger of the connection is the self-complacency of the superior, which in all matters of controversy will probably decide in its own favour."
>
> Edmund Burke

"We are moving," said Gordon Brown in January 2001, "from the old Britain of subjects, where people had to look upwards to a Whitehall bureaucracy for their solutions, to a Britain of citizens where, region to region, we are in charge." Whether the Chancellor was being ironic in his use of "we", who knows? But to any student of the Treasury during his era his apparent disowning of power was bizarre.

In the previous chapter I examined the half-hearted attempts to install elected government for hospitals, and even more half-hearted nods towards police and school trusts. The ambition in each case has been to circumvent existing institutions of local democracy, notably elected counties. The new localism was to be expressed through

Beacon Schools, "excellent" councils, three-star hospitals and the culture of "earned autonomy". None represented a real turning back of the centralism that had dominated relations between Whitehall and local government since 1997.

Yet there was one reform that escaped the centralist net early in Labour's first term and which was real. From it lessons can be learned. It revived the failed devolution of two decades earlier to Wales and Scotland and restored metropolitan government in Greater London. Ireland, Wales and Scotland were parts of the United Kingdom that had long sought varying degrees of autonomy. Wales had been formally incorporated into "England and..." under Henry VIII. Scotland joined England formally through Queen Anne's Act of Union. Whereas Scotland had long enjoyed a range of devolved powers, notably in law and education, Wales did not do so. There had been a Welsh Office only since 1964. Statutes and statistics referred to England and Wales as one entity.

Devolution acts for Scotland and Wales Acts passed in 1998. Within two years a Parliament and Executive was installed in Edinburgh, an Assembly and executive in Cardiff. There followed a directly elected mayor and assembly for London. An attempt was also made to devolve regional power to Northern Ireland. Though an executive was installed at Stormont (for the third time) it collapsed in 2003. All these reforms showed that it was possible to insert a devolutionist foot in the door of British centralism.

## London

The new constitutional measures were instantly met by predictable resistance within Whitehall. The Treasury pressed for devolved institutions to be largely deliberative. Accountability, especially for the spending of money, had to remain in Whitehall. In London the prospect of a left-wing mayor in the form of Ken Livingstone made this battle particularly fierce. Matters were resolved by extensive "Henry VIII" clauses allowing the centre to overrule mayoral decisions, and denying London any new taxing powers. The resulting Greater London Act was so bound up in restrictions as to be the longest ever passed by a British Parliament.

The London mayor is powerful in relation to the assembly but not in relation to Whitehall. He can plan for London's future and has proved a controversial campaigner for high-rise buildings. With regard to the police his powers are limited to appointing a police authority and to consultation. Yet one of his first acts was to defy the Home Office and recruit a thousand extra police officers, demanding a higher precept on the boroughs to pay for them. Normally the Home Office would have slapped down such profligacy from a local council or police authority. It did not do so in London, faced as it was with a clear mandate from a directly elected mayor. Something had changed.

The centre hit back elsewhere. The mayor's chief responsibility was for transport. Mr Livingstone appointed a high-profile American, Bob Kiley, as his transport commissioner and launched a new City and West End congestion charge. The Treasury had long been planning the privatisation of London's Tube infrastructure, leasing three groups of lines to two consortia at highly preferential terms. This saddled Londoners, whether as travellers or tax-payers, with £1 billion of subsidies a year. Mr Brown rejected Mr Livingstone's alternative proposal for bonds to be issued on the New York model. The scheme was working in cities round the world, but as with British Rail the Treasury could not tolerate anything "not invented here", even though bonds had once been a common feature of British local finance. Its plan cost some £500m in fees to set up and was financially crippling to the future Underground. Services deteriorated as soon as the new system was transferred to the private sector in 2003.

Yet direct election in London was a true localist innovation. Half-hearted efforts were made to extend the idea to towns and cities elsewhere. A heavily biased referendum system whereby cities could opt for a mayor resulted in only 12 taking office by 2004. Often eccentric, these individuals proved popular and most seemed destined for re-election, as was Mr Livingstone in 2004. Londoners declared that he "offered a stronger voice for London" and wanted him to have more, not less, power. After almost two decades with no democratic government, Londoners felt the breath of emancipation.

## Wales

Wales was different. Its people had voted in 1997 by the narrowest of margins – just over half of a 50 per cent turnout – for a devolved national assembly. The government refused to convert this limited mandate into an assembly with taxing or legislative powers. Its "ministers" were to be executive officers under a remaining Secretary of State for Wales. This impotence was widely derided. The Richard Commission in 2004 pleaded with London to give the assembly more power, which may yet happen.

That said, the new structure soon took on a personality of its own. The new first minister, Rhodri Morgan, was seen as Wales's figure-head, contrasting with the government's Secretary of State for Wales.

The assembly and its ministers tested their powers to the limit. They rejected the government's schools white paper and abandoned its school testing regime. There was even talk of a Welsh "baccalaureate". Two years later the assembly refused to accept foundation hospitals on their territory.

Perhaps the most vivid sign of the ballot attracting accountability was 2004 data indicating that Wales's health service had performed worse since devolution. This was blamed not on central government, which was in fact responsible, but on Mr Morgan. Democratic accountability was attaching to elected individuals. It was "biting".

Any sign of regional distinctiveness was reported prominently in the local media. This gave a Welsh dimension to public services which had been wholly lacking before. The assembly might be legally impotent, yet it was acquiring legitimacy. It became harder for central government to overrule. Opposition to devolution within Wales fell from 40 per cent in 1997 to 24 per cent in 2002.[49]

## Scotland

Scottish devolution was more clear. Under the Scotland Act 1998, the national parliament recovered much of the autonomy Scots local government had lost to London since the 1970s. The office of Secretary of State for Scotland was discontinued and its powers vested in a new First Minister and a cabinet. The parliament was given power to levy income tax of up to 3p in the pound, one it has yet to use. It could organise its own health service and public transport, run its own schools and universities, administer its own courts. Scotland diverged from London on such matters as care of the elderly, university tuition fees and teacher salaries.

Any visitor to Scotland can be in no doubt who rules it. The new parliament was abused and derided from the start, as are all devolved institutions. Nor was it helped by extraordinary cost overruns on its magnificent £400m parliament building. Yet the parliament soon became the forum of Scottish politics and government, supported by Edinburgh's prominence as one of Europe's most splendid cities. As John Curtice of Strathclyde University has commented, "Scots reaction to the disappointments of devolution is to demand more of it rather than less". The idea of reverting to rule from London is unthinkable. In Scotland the decentralist ball is rolling.

The reaction of Whitehall and Westminster to this devolution is well captured in an exchange between Mr Blair and the Liberal Democrats' Paddy Ashdown, recounted in the latter's diaries. The occasion was the Scots refusing to follow London in imposing higher university tuition fees. Mr Blair protested that Scotland "cannot do something different from the rest of Britain". Surely, said Mr Ashdown, that was the point of devolution. Mr Blair's response was instructive, "I am beginning to see the defects in all this devolution stuff."[50] A Whitehall official at the time told me that had Scots devolution been postponed to Labour's second term, it would never have proceeded. Downing Street now hated it as much as had the Treasury.

## Northern Ireland

Northern Ireland is usually omitted from debate on the British constitution. Yet it is part of the United Kingdom and has its story to tell. Thirty years of failure to establish a power-sharing local government at Stormont illustrates the folly of establishing regional rule in provinces with no shared political identity. Ulster's Unionists and

Nationalists were always too far apart to govern together. Northern Ireland was born of partition. It was the child of failed power-sharing. Not surprisingly its politics has rejected it ever since.

Yet even as devolved government was collapsing at Stormont in the 1970s, London proceeded with another flank of constitutional reform in Ulster. It abolished the old six counties as they would be "unnecessary" if Stormont were up and running. Subsidiary districts were left with little more than parish-style powers, though Belfast and Londonderry kept their grander city councils. Stormont did not happen, but county abolition did. As a result even at the most local level the entire province is ruled directly by "England". Ulster today is indeed a model of what Whitehall has in mind for the English regions. It has, at the last count, 20 ministries with a complete complement of officials. It has more civil servants per head than any other part of the UK, with higher public spending and a wide democratic deficit. It is no nearer self-government.

Yet while Stormont has failed, inter-communal power in Northern Ireland has indeed been "shared" on the 26 surviving district councils. The divided communities of Belfast and Londonderry elect councillors to their city halls where they work together, away from the bright lights and grandstanding of the direct-rule institutions of Stormont. British government has never noticed this. It has not sought to re-invigorate Ulster's political life by restoring its counties, or by granting more power to its cities and districts. It has preferred to rule by itself. Control is all.

Scots, Welsh and Northern Irish devolution received an incidental boost from the earlier failure of devolution in 1978. They received a regional block grant. This "Barnett formula", related to population and a historic starting-point, gave them more per head than English authorities, though they still had to rely on the Treasury for major project approvals. The Treasury rattles its sabre when any devolved executive threatens "excessive expenditure". But the block grant principle survives unscathed in all three regions, and the devolved responsibility that goes with it.

"Celtic fringe" localism went so far and no further. It is a measure of Westminster's approach that where regional identity was accepted in Scotland, Wales and Northern Ireland, other lessons of European regionalism were not. The customary two-tier subsidiary government within the regions was rejected. Whitehall seized on the existence of regional assemblies to pursue its campaign against counties. Having abolished them in Ireland it now abolished them in Wales and Scotland. Boundaries were redrawn to give just one tier of large unitary authorities.

Seen from below the effect was to diminish not reinforce local self-government. Most non-urban communities now found themselves answerable to more distant rule than ever before. Wales was reduced to 22 districts and Scotland to 32. This was a drastic reduction in local autonomy, putting the Celtic extremities among the least democratic territories in Europe, more so for the time being than England.

The people of Aberdovey, on the west coast of Wales, used to be a "district" with the neighbouring resort of Towyn, administering its own roads, social services and local planning. Schools and highways came under the historic county of Merioneth, in not-distant Dolgelly. Aberdovey is now part of a unitary authority based two hours' drive away in Carnarvon, not even within the former Merioneth. Local people have little more in common with Carnarvon than they do with Cardiff. As for whether the new structure is more efficient, ask any resident. Even the colour of the pier railings and state of public lavatories must be directed to Carnarvon. A democracy that was granted regionally was withdrawn locally.

Properly local government in Scotland, Wales and Ulster has long been the discarded wallflower at the devolution ball. Seen from above it is something from which local electors should always be "spared". Reform is always aimed at reducing "unnecessary" local government. Yet I once attended to a Brussels seminar at which officials spoke of Whitehall and "national parliaments" in similarly dismissive terms. Should not antiquated nation states be spared this unnecessary tier? I am sure Whitehall would not see things that way.

## England

The search for an "English dimension" to the devolution debate has consumed comment ever since 1997. The momentum came from those in government who feared that centralism was opening a vacuum in local accountability and that something was needed to fill it. The answer was to be a wholly novel concept in English geography, "regions".

The Tories had laid the ground. In 1994 they set up nine regional offices of Whitehall to strengthen and co-ordinate control over local authorities. Labour in Opposition protested that these offices were unaccountable and in 1995 proposed regional development agencies (RDAs) answerable to elected "chambers". These RDAs were duly launched in 1999 and, like all agencies of Whitehall, displayed extraordinary bureaucratic vigour, costing £1.8 billion by 2004. "Directorates" commanded salaries of £60-90,000 to co-ordinate, plan, prioritise, steer, skill, train and "develop" each other. The West Midlands agency opened offices in Chicago, Paris, Tokyo and San Jose. Something called the "East of England Development Agency" took on a sovereignty of its own. It sought meetings with "key figures, catalysts and landmark promoters". It was as if the British civil service, freed from the geographical disciplines of Whitehall, lost all self-restraint.

Labour's pledge of elected chambers for RDAs was soon forgotten. Accountability was to lie with boards handpicked by ministers. A majority of members must come vaguely from "business", including the chairman, with only a minority from local councils. The Treasury was determined to use these bodies as spearhead battalions of its planning machine, so long balked by obscurantist localism. For once Mr Prescott's aversion to local government and Mr Brown's aversion to democracy in any form were able to operate in tandem. The appointed regional offices were a perfect proxy for the suppression of the counties and the furthering of central control.

Localism across Europe has mostly had a strong regional element. The reason is simple. Germany, France, Italy and Spain are federations of ancient kingdoms, dukedoms and statelets. These identities survived, at least in local loyalty, into the 20th century. England has no such regional loyalty. Since the dawn of its history the subsidiary units of personal identity and local government have always been cities and shire counties, whether big ones such as Yorkshire and Kent or small ones such as Herefordshire or Rutland. Outside the big cities, the county remains the focus of local enthusiasm, commerce, tourism, sport and social networking. Even Whitehall officials have cottages in "Gloucestershire" and "Shropshire", not the South-West or the West Midlands.

Natives of Cheshire or Suffolk have no doubt. They regard adjacent Staffordshire or Essex as foreign country. To advocate a localism that ignores this and merges counties into a hodgepodge defies the basis of local democracy. It is classic top-down reform. Whenever such mergers have been tried, as in Hereford and Worcester, it has been resisted fiercely. New-fangled "counties", such as Humberside or Avon, do not take root. Such geographical engineering destroys the habits and associations that underpin identity. The "regions" of England are unlike those of southern Europe. They are like those of Scandinavia. They are counties.

One indication of this is that Whitehall's attempts to decentralise its administration have never agreed on what an English region is. One survey counted 100 different groupings of counties or bits of counties, invented by different government departments.[51] The latest eight "standard regions" have never won affection, lumping Gloucestershire with Cornwall, Cheshire with Cumbria and Buckinghamshire with Kent. No public consent was sought for these groupings.

In mapping new regional police forces in the 1970s, the Home Office fell back on a pre-Norman Hobbit-land of Mercia, Wessex and Dyfed. Even these were too local for Whitehall's standard regions. These fell back on compass points, on East Midlands or North-West, as Whitehall had fallen back on the French Revolution's use of rivers in naming its aborted metropolitan counties. All heavily bureaucratised organisations fall into the same trap. The National Trust even has a region called "Thames and Solent". Sovereign entities to which no one can put a name are reminiscent of Orwell's "Airstrip One" in '*1984*'s' Oceania. When a friend of mine was sent from London to rule the new region of "South-West" even he admitted that he would live in "Somerset".

In 2002 came a belated recognition that the RDAs lacked the democratic oversight once promised them. A white paper, 'Your Region, Your Choice', offered to replace the Treasury's boards of businessmen with elected members, but only if the relevant region wanted this in a referendum. And then only at a price. The price, to no one's surprise, was the total abolition of any subordinate counties. The new assemblies would be concerned only with economic development, housing, tourism and planning, and even then only in an "influencing role" on central government. Spending would be capped by the Treasury.

What happened next could not be equalled for cynicism. Mr Prescott suggested three regions as pilots: Yorkshire and Humberside, the North-West and the North-East. Here the Treasury had less interest in central control because there were fewer opportunities for economic development. But when it seemed that two of the three northern regions might reject Mr Prescott's half-hearted devolution he cursorily abandoned their polls. Initially only the North-East was to be allowed a vote on whether it should have a regional assembly.

This "region" is much the smallest and the one with the most local coherence. It is the "Geordie-land" of just two counties, Northumberland and Durham, to whom devolution was doing little more than restoring the powers they had enjoyed separately prior to the 1980s. Together with the old county boroughs of Newcastle, Gateshead, South Shields and Sunderland, here at least was a political entity that reflected local identity, on a par with French or German equivalents. Yet it did not occur to Mr Prescott that he was acknowledging the county case. Nor would he make the same status available to, for instance, Cornwall, which would undoubtedly have voted itself a "region".

The regional aspect of the new localism was as ham-fisted as the elected hospital boards. It might seem extraordinary that any electorate would decline a proffered involvement in its local affairs. The reason for the unpopularity of English regions can only be that they in no way corresponded to an identifiable area. People were offered a geographical entity of which they knew nothing, and at the expense of losing one to which they had been long attached, their county. As the Welsh and Scots had found, this sort of regionalism was anti-localist.

As of today only Scotland bears some resemblance to the regional governments of other European states, albeit without much subsidiary democracy. Yet Scotland is developing an autonomous political life, and demanding more devolution. The 1998 acts proved that democracy can be decentralised where politics so decides. This decentralisation stopped Scots and Welsh separatism in its tracks. John Major's thesis, borrowed from Lady Thatcher, that devolution would "lead to the break-up of the United Kingdom" was absurd. If anything it diminished such a risk. The Scottish and Welsh nationalists have never recovered from devolution.

Where government devolves real self-rule to territories that have popular recognition, autonomy takes root. Where no such entities exist, as in the English regions, it does not. Mention counties or cities as centres of local self-government on the European pattern and ministers will declare them "too small to be viable". Yet last August Mr Blair went to Athens to watch 200 sovereign nations parade before him into the Olympic stadium. A third of them were smaller, weaker or poorer than Kent or the West Riding of Yorkshire. Nobody told them they were non-viable.

# 5. State and Super-State

> Now you shall feel the strength of Tamburlaine
> And, by the state of his supremacy
> Approve the difference 'twixt himself and you.
>
> Christopher Marlowe

Nations need the apparatus of a central state. "The United Kingdom of Great Britain and Northern Ireland" is one nation and its people expect to see that reflected in an elected government. Its duties naturally embrace foreign affairs, defence, trade, competition, macro-economic policy, justice, law and order. To these are customarily added minimum standards in public health and social welfare.

Britain's government has many features of a monarchical state, mostly but not all ceremonial. Ministers owe allegiance to "the Crown" from the moment they are selected from Parliament. The Crown thus becomes synonymous with the government and its head, the prime minister. This makes available to him and ministers generally a most useful concept of royal prerogative. It is used with increasing facility to cover national security, official secrets and decisions on appointments, patronage and honours. The prerogative enables government to go to war without parliamentary approval. Crown "privilege", not to mention immunity, remains in place and is frequently cited in legislation. The all-embracing provisions of much local government legislation are known as "Henry VIII clauses". They amount to rule by decree.

Accountability to Parliament means that ministers must command a parliamentary majority. But in an age of party discipline, this makes most decisions self-legitimising. Only where governments push their backbenchers (or peers) too far does parliament offer a check. Most recent parliamentary rebellions have been against excessive executive power, as with the executive control of judges, a national police force, school restructuring, university autonomy and postal voting. It is significant that these checks were applied not by the Commons but by Britain's last shred of legislative pluralism, the House of Lords.

Few governments feel wholly at liberty to use their parliamentary majority to tear up core constitutional statutes, such as those on the status of the monarch and the regularity of parliaments. But the list of such protected statutes has become shorter under recent governments. "Quasi-constitutional" conventions were once changed only by Royal Commission or some other bipartisan device. In the 1960s, reform of both local government and the universities was delegated to Royal Commissions. Such caution was considered proper to Britain's informal constitution.

It has now been all but abandoned, often amid scenes of chaos. Attempts to reform the House of Lords, introduce regional government, abolish the Lord Chancellor and create a supreme court have been rushed and partisan. Constitutional change has been "plotted on the back of an envelope", according to the former minister, Robin Cook. All such reforms have been a shambles and none has yet been achieved. Never did Britain's safeguards of precedent and caution, such as they are, seem more important – or more threadbare.

The constitutional treatment of local government is a special case. To lawyers it is "a creature of the state". Its rights are as vulnerable to usurpation as was baronial and civic power in the past. Local councils may administer the majority of public services and do so under the aegis of a mass democracy of some 22,000 elected citizens. But all this is "at the pleasure of Parliament".

Local democracy can sometimes break down, especially when its constitutional updating is long neglected. As I discuss below, it has so atrophied in Britain that it now requires a leap of imagination to see it performing tasks considered normal elsewhere in Europe and America. In some cases the centre has felt obliged to intervene, as in Lambeth and Hackney in the 1990s. In other cases it has deliberately not done so. Kenneth Baker, as Mrs Thatcher's environment secretary in the 1980s, deliberately refused to intervene in Labour Liverpool, he told me, so that he could use it as proof of the awfulness of local government. It was the goose that laid a thousand centralist eggs.

Of the list of functions pertaining to a central state, the most important for local government is the setting of minimum standards. Ever since the health reforms of the 19th century this has been regarded as a proper duty of the national parliament, often opposing the perceived "rights" of local councils. But throughout the past century the centre has exercised this duty at arm's length. It has "required" tasks of the locality, and contributed to their cost. Plans for health and education were "to be prepared". Duties to provide care were imposed. Schools, clinics and housing was demanded. But a line was drawn as to how these requirements should be met and what priorities should be applied to meeting them. The state expected a healthy and an educated nation, but did not stipulate how health and education had to be achieved.

Across Europe social benefits tend to be standardised on a national basis. This is despite wide variations in local costs and prices. Those who get more for their pound by living in poor areas are considered lucky. But benefits involving the supply of services, the running of institutions and the exercise of professional discretion are regarded differently. The reason is obvious. No sensible state attempts to run every building and employ every official from its capital city. Central government cannot be sensitive to personal or communal needs, nor can it offer the institutional leadership which most welfare services require. Hence the devolution in most countries to local authorities of hospitals, schools, the care of young and old and the upkeep of public buildings.

Nor do most countries worry unduly about the size of the units administering such welfare. No European country is the same in history, politics or income disparity. Even the northern states regarded as most comparable with Britain deliver public services in units of widely varying size. In Germany most have an average population of 4m, Denmark of 500,000, Luxembourg of 400,000 and Scotland of 5m. In England, the government's ambition is that a viable policy unit for public services should be the whole country, of 50m people. Such is considered essential to achieve an equitable and efficient distribution of welfare.

For reasons that will by now be clear, I find Britain's position absurd. Central government must lay down minimum standards, and must orchestrate redistribution from rich areas to poor ones to make such minima attainable. But it need not intervene in their implementation to the degree it does. Whitehall's fastidiousness leaves foreign observers aghast. Its formulas for redistribution – an "index of multiple deprivation" informing a "local government finance formula grant distribution scheme" – involve mathematics far beyond lay comprehension.

As I discuss in the next chapter, fiscal redistribution does not require central policy-making and heavy-handed monitoring. The European trend has been in the other direction, away from ring-fencing and towards block grant. That government should be able to redistribute public resources between its citizens and yet allow them autonomy in using them is the sign of a mature democracy. It is a sign of trust.

Certainly central government must ensure that its standards are met and that its money is spent justly and equitably. Such audit customarily takes two forms: technical accountancy and political accountability. Britain respects the first far more than the second. Whitehall in the 1980s and 90s saw an explosion of professional audit. The blast extended across the landscape of local administration, claiming competence in matters once deep within the remit of local democracy. I see no way to correct this except to re-establish the supremacy of local government as such, to return to it far greater discretion in deciding spending priorities and monitoring them. Audit must be relocalised. It must be made the servant not the master of local government.

This will only be achieved by curtailing the extent of central inspection, notably the work of the Audit Commission. Councils should choose their own auditors and decide for themselves how far they wish that audit to stray into value for money. Best practice will dictate some uniformity, but diversity is the essence of autonomy. Partial and often distorted league tables are for journalists, not responsible government. Published reports and open debate should inform local electorates, not a council's ranking in a Whitehall pantheon. Government's job is to ensure proper procedure, not "proper" expenditure.

The centre must be the guardian of last resort of public justice. Citizens and groups must be able to appeal against decisions that affect them, even decisions of those they elected, where they infringe statutory requirements. They must be protected against corrupt and arbitrary government – local as well as central. This requires a body of administrative law, as yet inadequate in Britain. A classic instance is in town and country planning. In Britain appeal against a local decision, except over process, is to a minister, rendering the appeal little more than a sales pitch for central policy. Most countries, for instance France, enjoy an appeal to a tribunal independent of the executive. Such tribunals should exist in Britain.

I am a minimalist about all tiers of government. Free citizens need constantly to be on their guard against them. But I am particularly sceptical of the upper tier of government because it is the most detached from private citizens and, by experience, the least efficient. I share this scepticism with most Western states. Central power is so seductive that those driving it forward need curbing at every turn, preferably by formal constitutions. Nowhere should this curb be more firm than in matters of territorial autonomy. Otherwise Gibbon's Rome will be followed by Britain's welfare state, its fall "the natural and inevitable effect of immoderate greatness... as soon as time or accident had removed the artificial supports, the stupendous fabric yielded to the pressure of its own weight." It simply collapsed.

# 6. The Bite of the Franchise

> "We are interested solely in power. Not wealth or luxury or long life or happiness: only power, pure power."
>
> George Orwell, '1984'

I once met a man walking his dog in a small township in Connecticut, New England. He was a Wall Street banker and elected comptroller of the town council. Though a weekend visitor, he held the job with pride and took it seriously. One reason was that local taxes on his house were $20,000. He was currently wrestling with how to induce his fellow residents to pay for a new fire station.

My friend was about to attend a Town Meeting on the subject, a formal decision-taking event based on a show of hands. He would have to defend the cost of the building and possibly abandon it in favour of some other scheme. This was New England democracy at work, direct heir to English vestry democracy imported by the Pilgrim Fathers. Services were paid for and delivered at the point of use. The people of Connecticut would never have it otherwise. Any state or federal government that presumed to remove the fire service from the hands of the town would rerun the American revolution.

A fire dispute consumed Britain in 2002-4. Though fire services were notionally a local responsibility, pay, working terms and conditions, investment and regulatory standards were all central. The local government employers formed themselves into a national consortium for negotiating purposes but were overridden by a minister, John Prescott. Any decision they reached would have to be financed in large measure by the Treasury. As a result, the fire service had for decades been left unreformed and inefficient, a classic nationalised industry but one for which no one nationally took responsibility.

Nothing distinguishes systems of government so much as finance. In America, citizens pay directly for most services, and can usually see if they are not being delivered. In Britain the opposite is the case. The mayor of any American city can levy, more or less, whatever taxes he or she likes. A mayor can balance a property tax against a sales tax, or a hotel tax against a commuter tax. A director of development can offer to waive taxes in return for particular local benefits. In California citizens can vote a specific "proposition" to tax, or untax, themselves for defined purposes such as education or welfare.

Across Europe local tax regimes make widely differing contributions to the public sector. Property taxes are regarded as robust because they apply to fixed and visible assets. They are in use almost everywhere but to a far smaller extent than in Britain, where they are the only local tax. They comprise just 17 per cent of local revenue in Belgium, 14 per cent in Italy and Spain, and 10 per cent in France. Of other taxes, the most popular is income tax. In Scandinavia it forms at least a third of regional and local expenditure. Almost 100 per cent of Denmark's local revenue is from income tax. The relatively heavy "bite" that such a tax makes on middle class citizens encourages a far more vigorous local politics than in Britain.

A local business tax, whether on profits, turnover, property or payroll, is levied in most countries. In France businesses contribute half of local revenue. Company taxes are levied locally in Germany, Italy, Spain, Portugal and Luxembourg. Spain's "autonomous communities" are entitled to levy a rich array of local taxes, including on gambling, wealth, transfers, vehicles, fuel and property. Individual municipalities can tax property, businesses, construction sites and motor vehicles. Local taxation in Italy since the 1990s has formed the bedrock of democratic reform. In municipalities, locally raised revenues went from 15 per cent of total revenue in 1991 to 45 per cent at the end of the decade (the rest coming from central government). Over the same period, the proportions in Britain were reversed.

The European Charter of Local Self-Government, signed by Britain in 1997, recommends that local revenue should be roughly commensurate with local responsibility, and should be within the democratic control of local councils. It should also be of a "diversified and buoyant nature". The Council of Europe recommends that councils should not be dependent on just one tax. These principles have been ignored by every modern British government.

British local authorities gain income from a levy on domestic property, based on eight bands of market valuation, covering an average of just 25 per cent of their spending. Other local revenues may come from rents, fees, parking and motoring fines. The remaining 60-70 per cent comes from central grants. Those grants include the old business property tax, now centralised and returned to councils as part of the general grant formula. Domestic property taxes tend to suffer from acute "fiscal drag", revenue tending to lag behind the spending dependent on it, and having to be supplemented more and more from central resources. Thus over the course of the 1990s local taxes fell to just 4 per cent of public sector revenue, as against 46 per cent in Sweden, 18 per cent in France and 13 per cent in Germany.

Estimates of how much of their activities councillors can consider discretionary, that is not required by central government, vary widely. The usual figure is between 5 and 15 per cent. But on this depend such high-profile services as libraries, the arts, parks and the local environment. The steady decline in such resources also means that any overspending by a council on statutory services requires often massive rises in local taxes. A 1 per cent overspend requires, on average, a 4 per cent rise in tax. This has led to council taxes rising 60 per cent in real terms since 1997. This further drives councils into conformity with government targets and discourages innovation.

The level of council tax is now widely treated as the responsibility of central government. This state of affairs is unique to Britain. Nothing better indicated this than the return in 2004 of a Tory measure hated and derided by Labour in Opposition, the council tax "cap". For 13 years the Conservative government had not dared allow councils the right to set their property taxes at will. Labour promised to end this "crude" rate-capping. For five years it held off, but fast rises in public sector spending, especially on salaries, began to break local budgets and generate council tax "revolts".

The revolts were directed at central not local government. The centre duly buckled. In the spring of 2004 Mr Prescott's junior minister, Nick Raynsford, declared that "we expect local authorities to budget prudently; unfortunately some haven't." This was the Mrs Thatcher of a decade earlier. Six councils found their rates capped, some of them after their tax demands had been printed and distributed. In the case of Newcastle the declared overspend was less than the cost of reissuing the demands. A general cap was then signalled for 2005.

The government also took the Thatcher parallel a stage further. As she had published her 'Alternatives to Domestic Rates' in 1981, a precursor to the poll tax, Mr Blair in 2002 announced a "balance of funding" review, to seek options to replace the council tax. No sooner had this inquiry completed work in June 2004 than Downing Street panicked. The prospect of any reform that might increase taxes on middle-class home owners was declared anathema. The inquiry saw its report dumped on yet another inquiry, told not to report before a general election. Mr Blair could not even bring himself to reform the most pressing flaw in council tax, the £350,000 threshold on the highest tax band. With soaring house prices in the South-East this meant that a quite modest homeowner was paying the same local tax as a millionaire. It rendered the council tax uncannily similar to the poll tax.

An old saying held that the British "paid their taxes in sorrow and their [local] rates in anger". The more visible a tax the more the public will dislike it, but equally the more it will carry democratic bite. In America local taxes for local services generate democratic activity. Nothing galvanised New York politics in the 1980s so much as the astronomical (by London standards) tax rises imposed on New Yorkers by their bankrupt mayors. Break that link and accountability starts to wander upwards, with ministers feeling ever more obliged to hold them down. As a result local taxes in Britain are among the lowest anywhere.

In the last chapter we saw the functions of the central state towards local government as to fix minimum standards and redistribute resources. A study for the 2004 Balance of Funding Review found that across Europe there was surprisingly little correlation between these functions and the degree of local autonomy. Most governments found themselves ready to give substantial money to local government without requiring detailed control over how it was spent.[52]

The key to this liberalism lay in the block grant principle. In these countries the grant either takes the form of single tranches of money or, as in Spain, giving local government access to a share of certain national taxes. This principle is not foreign to Britain. It applied under the 1958 block grant system, which remained robust until the 1980s, and continues in the Barnett subventions to Wales and Scotland. Any tax regime that tries to equalise resources across disparate territories will involve complexity and is unlikely to be wholly equitable. Grappling with such complexity has been the stuff of government since the Middle Ages. It is customarily resolved through mechanisms of redistribution that need not crush local autonomy.

English local councils must have full block grant restored to them if any trust is to return to relations between the centre and locality. In the midst of the debate over the new localism, in July 2004 the Treasury offered Local Area Agreements to 62 experimental authorities in 21 areas. This was intended to compress 60 or so defined revenue streams to local government from 17 government departments into just three "themed pots". These would cover children and young people, "safer and stronger communities" and "healthier communities and old people". Police and education would remain outside the pots. But there was to be no virement between the silos, except possibly for one lucky council to see what might happen. The change applied to just 9 councils and was described as being "experimental". All this was hardly a return to 1958.

I agree with the suggestion of McLean and McMillan that the block grant formula should be "coarse" rather than over-sophisticated.[53] It must be predictable to councils and comprehensible to a layman, and therefore fixed "not by a department of government but by an independent commission". Governments are incapable of not distributing central resources so as to aid their own political interest. This function, which I would give to a Local Democracy Commissioner (see below) would be to assess local needs and resources and allocate central grant from an overall budget. This, and this alone, should be the basis of central allocation to localities.[54]

The re-establishment of block grant is not all. Common sense, equity, security and the European Charter all point to local councils having a far wider portfolio of taxes than one on domestic property. By general agreement local taxes should in some sense reflect ability to pay, whether through an income tax or at least some sort of occupancy tax. Local income taxes are far more widespread abroad than most Britons realise. Taxation should also embrace local businesses, in some form. This might also cover hotels, farming, tourism, gambling, vehicle duty and entertainment. Urban councils such as Westminster are already receiving half their locally-based revenue from traffic control. Central government levies numerous "stealth" taxes. There is no reason why local government should not do so too.

For local democracy to revive, local revenue must rise. This will be unpopular. In the mid-1980s local taxes in Britain covered 60 per cent of their spending, well above the European average. This has been more than halved. It must be engineered back up again, to give local voting more bite. This rise in local taxation should in some degree be "progressive", falling more on rich than poor. It should also be covered by wider local options, including local referendums on exceptional council tax rises. One such vote, in Milton Keynes in 1999, was strongly in favour of a higher tax. Evidence from Scandinavia suggests that where local communes sense their money is going to a worthy cause, they will vote for increases. They will not do so when local taxes are seen as merely relieving pressure on the Treasury.

In this I wholly endorse the detailed proposals to reform local taxation by Tony Travers and Lorena Esposito in their 2004 Policy Exchange pamphlet *Nothing to Lose But Your Chains*. Their mix of property, business and local income taxes is similar to that in place elsewhere in Europe. It makes sense.

The lesson of the rest of Europe – and of devolution so far within the United Kingdom – is that central grant should revert to a single grant undifferentiated by service. Once it arrives at county or city halls, it should pass into the hands of local democracy, to whom it should render its account. That is the way to get able people to serve on local councils, when their taxes are at risk. It is democracy not as carrot but as stick. My Connecticut banker understood.

# 7. The Localist Programme

> "The much-boasted constitution of England was noble for the dark and slavish times in which it was erected... That it is now imperfect, subject to convulsion, and incapable of producing what it seems to promise is easily demonstrated,"
>
> Thomas Paine

The 1969 Royal Commission on Local Government developed a concept called circles of identity. To calculate these circles, staff jokily invented a "Marbella test". One Briton meets another on a Mediterranean beach and asks from where he comes. If he is from Scotland, Wales or Northern Ireland, that will be the first answer. If he is from England, that will not be mentioned but rather a city or a county. In the case of big cities, Leeds, Birmingham, Manchester, that answer will suffice. But in smaller towns and villages there will be two answers, "Ludlow in Shropshire" or "Scarborough in Yorkshire" or "a little village in Staffordshire, you won't have heard of it."

These responses mean something. They indicate a sense of place. They declare community – and communities – and thus the realm in which social and political intercourse makes sense. Citizens of cities have always owed allegiance and security to their civic leaders. Inhabitants of smaller towns and rural communities owe a double allegiance, to their local village or municipality and to their wider county. This tiered identity is reflected in the novels of George Eliot and Trollope, as it is in the scripts of the *Archers* and *Coronation Street*. These are "the ties that bind". (This did not stop the 1969 Commission advising their abolition.)

Local government has always represented such tiers. The great cities were incorporated by charter and enjoyed privileges of self-government back to the Middle Ages. Shire counties were centres of feudal and baronial privilege, later a patchwork of boroughs, parishes and vestries. This pattern was robust even as local government democratised during municipal and county government reforms of the 19th century. Cities of more than 150,000 people became unitary "county boroughs". The rest of the United Kingdom was governed two-tier, by county and subsidiary district councils. The system worked, as it worked across Europe, because it broadly corresponded to popular sentiment.

For reasons that I still find puzzling all British governments since the 1980s have struggled to break this system. It is as if the existing cities and counties represented some dark intimation of rebellion. Within them lurked loyalties and lives of their own and they were opposed alike by Conservative and Labour regimes. The 1970 Conservative government merged some counties and converted big cities into "metropolitan counties". It mimicked the French revolutionaries and gave the new urban areas names from rivers – Avon,

Humberside, Tyne and Wear and Merseyside – as if to wash away the sins of the unmentionable cities. They lasted a mere ten years.

A review under Sir John Banham in the 1990s roamed the nation with maps and scissors, making recommendations with which ministers constantly meddled. It was, he said, "a time of blood, sweat and tiers". Berkshire was abolished and divided into three unitary authorities, neighbouring Buckinghamshire survived as a two-tier county. Herefordshire and Worcestershire were merged in 1974 and then demerged, the one as a unitary authority the other not. By the time of John Prescott, the citizens of Totnes in Devon were told that in future they would be citizens of no such entities, but of South Hams in the South-West Region.

Whitehall's fixation was that any "local government" (other than on an island) must be of a fixed size. There may be tiny states enjoying complete sovereignty elsewhere in the world, but Whitehall knows not of them. The USA has most-purpose authorities varying from 1,000 people to 1m. The plenipotentiary State of New Hampshire has only half the population of the capped and cribbed county of Hampshire in England. Scandinavia has shown that even the smallest communities can run a successful and equitable welfare state. French communes employ local police. Danish municipalities run primary schools. Swedish communities run primary health care. German mayors borrow money and control economic development. Viability is what a democrat wants it to be. Sub-contracting can handle economies of scale. Each family does not employ its own gardener.

The map of local government in the United Kingdom that existed prior to 1974 was a good one. The map survives in essence to this day and there is no good reason for tearing it up. It should form the foundation of democratic revival. Where in Scotland, Wales and Northern Ireland the counties have been destroyed, they should be reinstated. (Wales's local press has never abandoned its county nomenclature.) The structure answers to the Marbella test.

England has no need of regional assemblies. There are regional aspects to economic development but they are properly central. Major roads, airports and power stations require central initiative, but they cannot require the overblown Whitehall outposts now erupting in Guildford, Bristol, Manchester, Newcastle and elsewhere. Meanwhile counties and major cities must have restored to them the functions they enjoyed as recently as the 1970s. These include planning, roads, secondary schools, environment, leisure and culture. There should again be police authorities, as there are in French communes. The new joint-authority police forces have proved less efficient than smaller county forces (see chapter three). Police is the most local of services. The present large command centres have drawn staff off the streets and out of the cities. They have not delivered crime reduction or public satisfaction, only bureaucracy.

The counties should also be given what Morrison wanted for them in the 1940s and what the rest of Europe has given them, the running of health services. The NHS has served its course. Decentralisation should be real. The counties should also take over the prisons and probation services, together with youth employment and training. All these functions would be conducted where appropriate in collaboration with adjacent cities. In effect, counties should be reinstated as Whitehall's regions.

There will be the familiar howls of anguish. Surely county and city councillors are far too parochial and incompetent to handle such vital services? Surely this will increase bureaucracy? To this I make two replies. First, they could not be more incompetent or bureaucratic than the London offices set up to oversee or supplant their work at present. It is central government, not local, that has seen spending rising fastest and scandals proliferate most shockingly over the past two decades. Second, how is it that British public servants, permanent and elected, must be regarded as more incompetent than those who handle these services in other European countries, all registering higher levels of public satisfaction than in Britain? I cannot accept that those who already stand for and already work in local government are "all incompetent". Nor should a handful of poor London councils, so long the exemplars for London political commentators, be seen as typical.

Bringing new functions under county and city government would more than treble local budgets and bring them a new swathe of professional involvement. Thousands more people would feel they had a stake in their local institutions and services. Experience overseas overwhelmingly suggests that public services are more responsive and more efficient where this applies.

Above all planning must be restored to the county tier. The 2004 Planning and Compulsory Purchase Act is the most truly anti-democratic measure passed by any recent cabinet. Determining the pattern of land-use is a classic community duty and removing it the mark of authoritarianism. County structure planning had its faults and counties were not always strong in combating corrupt local development controllers. This is an argument for the reform of county planning, not its abolition. Planning remains the principle engine of local democracy, and rightly so. Regulating the character of one's community is the essence of localism. It is what makes people angry, and their anger is the fuel of democracy.

Personal public services are a different matter. The maxim has long been that they should be run as close as possible to the point of delivery. The local government minister, Nick Raynsford, has even stipulated that responsibility for such services be "transferred downwards to the lowest level at which it can effectively be discharged" and that this is best done "at the local or neighbourhood level".[55] He did not say what this meant. What is incontrovertible is that modern technology and subcontracting enable public services to be delivered at a lower tier than now.

I would copy Scandinavia and delegate most personal services with the exception of health to the lowest identifiable tier of local government. In England that means a city, a town or a parish council, what abroad are municipalities and communes. Such councils, however small, should be seen as self-governing entities for the services they can reasonably supply. This means services that are directly personal, where contact between supplier and user is more effective because each in some degree knows the other. This applies with the parson and the teacher, why not with the doctor and the social worker?

These municipalities and parishes should be charged with caring for whatever gives a community its pride and visual character. This means the running of primary school buildings and old peoples' homes, nurseries and day-care centres, clinics and surgeries. It would include the upkeep of what is in most places the most important historic building, the parish church, together with the market hall and sports centre. Nothing is more depressing about local Britain than the dreary appearance of such buildings compared with their European counterparts, dreary because no longer the responsibility of local people.

Responsibility would be vested in a multiplicity of town and village councils. No one pattern would apply everywhere. Diversity and its resulting innovation is the strength of such devolution elsewhere. The requirement is only that these be identifiable communities to which residents feel a sense of loyalty. In most cases the effect would be to make tens of thousands of institutions – such as primary schools, police stations and care centres – more or less self-governing, in the manner desired by many of Whitehall's pseudo-localist ideologues. Their governors would be drawn from their immediate community. Their budgets would be strictly local, as would the raising of additional sources of income.

The virtue of such a pattern is that it involves no great upheaval. Across England these councils are incorporated already as town, borough and parish councils. The only casualties – the only structural radicalism in my programme – would be the larger rural district councils, which would be subdivided into their municipalities and parishes. Each county scheme for devolution should be vetted by the Local Democracy Commission, which would also vet the local fiscal regime. As I explain in chapter six, I see no problem in tax variation between local authorities, even ones as small as parishes. Council taxes vary between districts, why not between parishes? They do elsewhere without revolution.

In urban areas the pattern is likely to be different, because loyalty tends to be to the city as a whole. Even so, most countries are moving towards sub-municipal democracy. Italian law requires neighbourhood councils in towns of more than 40,000 people. Germany has a similar law requiring elected councils in cities of more than 95,000. Sweden, Norway and the Netherlands have similar provisions. In America and

Canada, "business improvement districts" have extended community action to inner areas. Businesses elect representatives with power to levy taxes on each other. All such systems honour the conclusion of the American historian, Robert Dahl, that "there is no evidence of any significant economies in city government attributable to larger size".

British governments have nodded in this direction. There is a move to set up urban parishes to parallel rural ones. The government's "new deal for communities" proposes elected community forums, though these are purely consultative. Ad hoc committees have been formed for housing action areas, urban partnerships and new schools. Such groups tend to rise and fall in response to single-issue emergencies. They are to protest or promote rather than engage in continuous advocacy.

A few places have seen more substantive structures, not always with success. An attempt at neighbourhood government in London's Tower Hamlets ended in chaos, admittedly in one of Britain's toughest areas. Birmingham's new districts are proving more successful. The city is divided into 11 areas, each with a committee composed of its elected councillors, a director and a multi-service team. These are urban parishes along lines that should be applied everywhere, administering refuse collection, street quality, libraries and leisure. Birmingham hopes to extend the remit of its districts into education, health care and police. Beneath this district level is a further network of some 70 consultative neighbourhood councils. The structure builds on local democracy rather than supplanting it, and appears robust.

Everyone likes to believe they live in a "village". The belief is usually a fantasy. No urban or suburban community is as contained and claustrophobic as a real village. But there is resonance in the word. Hence the popularity of such village dramas as the Archers and Coronation Street. They are an antidote to Robert Putnam's call to arms, 'Bowling Alone', which warned of the decline, even in America, of the "habit of association". Scout troops were collapsing because nobody wanted to run them while the number of policemen, guards and lawyers had doubled in 30 years. The warning had Putnam invited to chat to Bill Clinton at Camp David, probably the highest compliment ever paid to a localist.

I believe that most Britons would gladly barter time, convenience and perhaps even their taxes for greater control over their immediate surroundings. Like my banker in chapter six, I would forego an evening a week to exert some power over the management of my local street, my park, my library and my clinic. If Swedish communities can enjoy this power, why not British ones? Why are Britons not allowed custodianship of so much as a lamp-post or a paving stone? The only scope allowed my neighbourhood at present is to hire its own security guards.

Britain should take its lead not just from Europe's localist present but from its own localist past. This is rooted in a communalism that long predates the democratic age. The historian, Carl Bridenbaugh, wrote of early 17th-century England, "Anyone who reads manorial records cannot fail to be astonished at the extensive participation of nearly every adult male in local affairs. Sooner or later, through appointment by manorial courts, the artificer, the copyholder, the poor husbandman and even the day labourer were called upon."[56] These citizens had to serve as jurymen, dog catchers and temporary constables. Through the organism of the vestry, "nearly all males in the rural parish, officers and servants, learned the rudiments of being governed and, to some extent, of governing."

This extended to local taxation. The town of Brighton in 1618 agreed at a meeting to levy variable local taxes on “landsmen” and “seamen” to defray local expenses. A local income tax was levied by a committee of churchwardens and the “chief of the town”. Nor was there any lack of employees to pay. The town ran bailiffs, inspectors of markets, harbour masters, street sweepers, pavers, constables and fire wardens. As for the size of these early local authorities they were diverse “in area, in population and in constitutional form: heterogeneity not uniformity was their salient characteristic”. The functions of these bodies were not much different from those I would expect of them today: the administration of local welfare, law and order, the care of the sick and elderly and, most important, primary education.

My prescription could hardly be simpler. It accepts unitary local government in English cities, but with two tiers in rural areas, of county councils and subsidiary municipalities and parishes. This is as has been the case for a century past. It reflects the local sentiments and loyalties of people nationwide. It has diversity without complexity. It is proven abroad. But how to make it happen?

# 8. The Big Bang

> I see you stand like greyhounds in the slips,
> Straining upon the start. The game's afoot;
> Follow your spirit.
>
> Shakespeare, *Henry V*

Gradualism will not answer to this need. Centralism is a process of remorseless stealth which infects all the processes of state. It has consumed both Conservative and Labour parties in power and goaded them into "something must be done" even in Opposition. While all pay lip service to localism, nobody practises it. Each step forward is followed by two back. There may be a consensus that Britain is an overcentralised state, but there is none on how to counter it.

Localism requires a Big Bang like the one visited on Britain's financial services in 1986. Big ideas need big stages on which to capture the public imagination and the commitment of leaders. Otherwise they never happen. Marginal changes in competition policy would never have transformed the City of London. It needed an explosion.

My revolution does not require a "written constitution" beloved of most political reformers. I have no doubt it would benefit from one. I agree with Ferdinand Mount that a proper constitution "can animate a society with a sense of what is right, and instil in government an understanding of the proper limits to the exercise of power."[57] But I am eager to keep this simple. Localism needs no great legislative upheaval, more a change in the attitude of mind of those who order local government from Westminster and Whitehall in London. It requires a mass divestment of central power similar to that which decentralised Denmark in 1970 and France in 1982. Both countries had similarities with modern Britain, the one social democrat in tradition, the other highly centralised in its administration. Both reformed themselves overnight. Both reforms worked.

There is another reason for a localist Big Bang. All constitutional change comes at a price. It involves that dread of the modern politician, losers. If localism is not carried forward as a grand package, losers will kill it. Each disadvantaged individual will appear as "everyman". Bad cases mean no reform. Low turnouts in mayoral elections argue against giving mayors more power. The poor quality of parish councillors is used against parish devolution. One corrupt local planner is an argument against all local planning. Above all, decentralised tax raising will increase some people's taxes even if it decreases those of others. Tax cuts are always silent but tax rises shout from the rooftops.

The form of the Big Bang would be simple. It would remove from existing local authorities overnight the mass of central interventions that have grown up over the past two decades. Down would come the policy silos. Out would go Whitehall's ad hoc agencies, task forces and initiatives. This can be done by executive order and would save colossal sums of money. The only areas requiring statutory intervention would be the delegation to counties of health services.

The biggest bang would blow away Whitehall's central and regional bureaucracy for monitoring central grants and targets. This would mean tearing up central performance regimes for local government and the apparatus of earned autonomy. Autonomy would become a fact, not a reward. Ring-fenced grants would be replaced with single block grants. Council staff would regain the freedom to experiment and the freedom to fail. Councillors and their electors would realise that what they said and did made a difference.

On a due date I would stage in every county, city and parish in England a "bonfire of controls" similar to that staged by the incoming Tory government in 1951. The bonfire would be a real one. Police chiefs, head teachers, doctors, hospital administrators and council executives would truck their input of Whitehall circulars, instructions and memoranda to a prominent site and burn them. In future each Whitehall department would be allowed one communication a year with any town hall.

This dismantling of centralism must coincide with a rebuilding of localism. Though most of the requisite institutions are in place, in the form of elected county, city, town and parish bodies, they are enervated and demoralised. But they are not dead. They need new blood and new talent to enable them to win public confidence as they go about their enhanced duties and wield their new freedoms. This especially applies where they mean to levy taxes on their fellow citizens. Since the perceived inadequacy of local councillors is the most commonly cited argument against localism, this shortcoming must be confronted head-on.

I believe strongly that the most effective way of reviving localism is through direct election. This might take the form either of a single elected mayor or county governor on the London (and American) model, or of a party list headed by a named candidate for each executive office. A study by Anna Randle of the 12 mayors introduced by the government's tentative mayoral reform 'Mayors Mid-term' (NLGN) shows a remarkably positive outcome. Randle shows that the mayors have proved popular and are likely to win re-election. They have disproved the many charges laid against the idea, that they would lead to confusion, corruption and autocracy. They are less partisan, more representative of their communities and certainly more prominent in local leadership than their party predecessors. Randle concludes, "they have not been a disaster and at their best they can be judged a success". They merit far more widespread dissemination.

Above all direct election yields the first requirement of open democracy, which is name recognition of representatives. A survey for NLGN taken just 18 months after mayors were elected showed them already enjoying almost two thirds recognition (and 73 per cent in the North East) against just 25 per cent of even the most longstanding council "leaders". In France and Germany, 80-90 per cent of people can name their mayor. This recognition adds potency to the office, giving the mayor a semi-independent political base. He or she has an electoral power that can help the community barter with the centre. I hasten to add that while localism would benefit from such an innovation it does not depend on it.

What is clear is that a Big Bang of this sort must commence with an electoral mandate from an incoming government, similar to that which drove the French reform of 1982 and the Scandinavian free communes. This would require a party ready to say to local government, you will be "forced to be free", and to local people, you will be "forced to be responsible". What form each county's localism takes would be for councils to discuss with their electors and with the Local Democracy Commissioner. As with 19th-century reform, the centre would require proposals and plans to achieve declared goals. Its stipulations should be general, that councils be in place, that named individuals be recognisable as accountable officers and that a framework of checks and balances be set up. This should apply at each tier of government.

Crucial to the success of a Big Bang is public information. Organising the first "festival of democracy" should be a national occasion, involving among other things the "coronation" of some 100,000 parish councillors as newly empowered local representatives. Local citizens should be left in no doubt that their system of government is going to change. The change will involve them taking greater responsibility for their environment and services. They must be left with no excuses if they refuse to participate. Localism tends to involve, most immediately and controversially, variations in local taxes. Such variations concentrate the democratic mind. That is the franchise biting. That is what drives people to vote.

Though such a programme might seem radical, it is no more than a return to liberties enjoyed by local communities in the past. Other than in the special case of health, these are hardly more extensive than existed as recently as the 1970s. They might be expressed through parishes and elected mayors, but these are hardly "un-British". I would even consider a measure of compulsion. We compel each other to sit on juries, a task which might be delegated to judges. We do so because we believe ordinary citizens have a compulsory role to play in local justice. In Tudor times this compulsion extended into all of public administration, across the whole range of local services. Many European countries expect tax-payers to vote, even if they register a blank. To attend a ballot hardly seems the most onerous of public obligations.

I have suggested a Local Democracy Commissioner and commission. This body would be independent of central government, charged with implementing the Big Bang. It would negotiate with counties and cities to determine their internal constitutions and electoral arrangements. It would vet schemes of devolution to parishes and monitor schemes for local taxes. It would assume the role of local government audit. It would, in other words, be the impresario of the localist revival.

# 9. The Enemy

> I was still cursed with my duality of purpose; and, as the first edge of my penitence wore off, the lower side of me, so long indulged, so recently chained down, began to growl for licence
>
> R.L.Stevenson, *Dr Jekyll and Mr Hyde*

The enemies of localism are people. The 20th-century centralisation of British public life has been conducted by ministers and officials, partly out of instinct, and partly for reasons. It is not fanciful to see them as descendants of the monarchical court. Since the reign of the Tudors, centralism has been the default mode of British government. Elizabeth's counsellors, struggling to assert her authority over a rebellious nation, were the true architects of today's state. They ordered every nuance of public life, from troop levies and church liturgy to the weight of cloth and the width of streets.

Most governments that fail to live up to public expectations do not really care. They are corrupt or poor or stupid. I would not say this of British government. I know politicians who are vain and ambitious but none is in politics for personal gain. Most sincerely try to "do the state some service", often at a cost to their careers and family life. The so-called welfare consensus has been safe in their hands. It is this that makes their centralism so morally entrenched.

The one belief they all share is that they are plenipotentiary. They believe their job is to set Britain, even the world, to rights. They will not admit that others, even if publicly elected, might do the job better. The ghost of the old "ruling classes" hovers over them. Only the French have their equal in arrogance. This attitude has slowly removed British government from the bedrock of public consent. Britain's democratic deficit is not a cliché but real.

There is no doubt of the moving spirit behind this process over that past two decades. Centralism is the ruling creed of the most powerful institution of modern government anywhere, the British Treasury. It has captured the policy of governments, making and breaking ministers and commanding the careers of officials. It has been, in my opinion, the worst department of state. Excellent at managing the economy – its chief function it has been truly appalling at managing the public sector. Its officials have little or no experience of such work yet ooze contempt for those who do, and enjoy the power to make that contempt effective. A study of the Treasury in the 1980s[58] depicted its officials as brilliant but aloof, fanatical in their conviction that they and only they know how to make the public sector tick. The "outside world" was a City bank, as it still is.

The Treasury has orchestrated most of central government's recent disasters. It sabotaged the poll tax and devastated all attempts at decentralising the NHS.[59] Its officials (not ministers) wrecked British Rail privatisation, undermined the Child Support Agency, made a fiasco of the British Library and blew an astonishing £500m in fees trying to privatise the London Tube. Their handling of public sector computer procurement has been stupefyingly expensive. Yet the institution and its denizens need never admit mistakes or answer for errors. Spending departments do that. The turmoil of Whitehall's "cultural revolution" in the 1990s felled ministers and agency chiefs, but left the Treasury untouched. As for local government, it has persistently fought all efforts to give it autonomy or fiscal licence. It renders laughable any claim that local government has some monopoly on incompetence or waste.

The Treasury embodies the rationalist fallacy, that a clever mind can handle the waywardness of human nature. At no point has it limited itself to being a "bureau of the budget" in the American fashion, guarding the public purse. Since the days of Lord Lawson it has sought to command every area of government policy. Kant might hold that "from the crooked timber of mankind no straight thing was ever made", but that is not the Treasury view. It tries to straighten the public sector daily. It acts as if government is science not art, and politics an obscene irrelevance. To such a body subsidiary autonomy can only be anathema.

But there is a wider centralist constituency than just the Treasury. London's political and administrative elite regards itself as a set apart. In the 40 years between the two editions of Anthony Sampson's 'Anatomy of Britain' what is most remarkable is how little has changed. To the rulers of Whitehall and Westminster, Britain beyond the boundaries of inner London is mostly a place of relaxation and retreat, a land of second homes, university towns and sporting venues. Such people will know their way round New York, Paris and Rome. They will trumpet the piazzas of Venice and the chateaux of the Dordogne. They will rarely have visited Manchester, Birmingham or Newcastle.

Provincial England was politically strong in the 19th century and well into the 20th but has lost its clout. Few legislatures echo their hinterland as little as does the British Parliament. MPs no longer live in the places they represent. The patronage-based House of Lords is overwhelmingly metropolitan. When the Civil Service was fashioned after the Northcote-Trevelyan report in 1854 it was as a corps d'elite to protect government from the corruption of politicians. It was also a counterweight to local power, that of city corporations and vestries. With the flowering of the welfare state, centre and locality fought a titanic battle over who should run it, and the centre won.

Today the centre has a professional interest in sustaining that victory. It is supported by an artillery of statutes and "Henry VIII" schedules and annexes. It can field a 60,000-strong army of quangos and task forces, many with their own outposts and garrisons in the Whitehall regions. These have mercenaries in reserve. Centralism has brought into being an array of accountants, lawyers, bankers and management consultants. A third of the income of some big accountancy firms is now from government. The mills and factories that once towered over central Leeds are replaced by the offices of PricewaterhouseCoopers. Its partners are no less a burden on the citizens of Leeds as ever were the millowners.

To these people the idea that Britain, or at least England outside London, might be able to organise its own public services is not so much unthinkable as unthought. As members of the upper middle class, they support the universalisation of modern culture as monopolised by capital cities. Provinces are places to be visited not for themselves, as an Italian visits an Italian city or a Frenchman a French province. They are visited as and when they ape London.

This is customarily as venues for art galleries, festivals and Cities of Culture (funded by a generous "national" lottery).

No British MP would consider being a civic leader. Reasonably competent MPs rarely need to take their lead from local opinion. Equally no council leader would think of challenging for ministerial office, as in America. No local chief executive would be considered qualified to head a Whitehall department. Central and local career structures are distinct vertically as well as geographically. I well remember a Whitehall permanent secretary returning from a county council visit shocked to find the people whom he had been patronising for years "were, you know, quite impressive – it's amazing."

This metropolitanism is hugely potent. It is the glue of centralism, of people who know one another, trust one another and do not trust those whom they do not know. This glue has seen British government through crisis after crisis, most of them self-generated. It displays what Bernard Crick calls "fear of politics" and Jerry White "fear of voting". It is terrified by any manifestation of popular will, it sought to stop the 2003 anti-war rally in London because it might damage the grass in Hyde Park. It sees no reason to dissolve itself at the whiff of grapeshot from some localist fad.

The metropolitan network is further reflected in that ever present mirror, the media. The press and broadcasting are now democracy's alternative parliament. Since British news organisations are London-based they form a natural centralising force. Staff live in the metropolis. They meet politicians and officials and share their assumptions. A collective contempt towards localism is palpable. The BBC Today programme used to run each summer a competition for listeners to send in tales of municipal absurdity, mostly to do with (centrally imposed) health and safety rules. Because the political class lives mostly in north London it also assumes that all local government is like north London's. It is not.

The Victorian press was once a fierce defender of local autonomy. The Leeds Mercury, Manchester Guardian and Birmingham Daily Press would rail against the imposition of London government on local institutions, usually with snide references to how much worse things were done in France. In 1848 the Leeds Mercury resisted a new Public Health Bill as an offence against "their municipal institutions – the boast, the characteristic of England and the bulwark of her liberties."[60] Today such papers would be demanding to know why local standards are not the same as standards nationwide.

National media comment is never biased in favour of 'laissez faire'. An American president would not answer a question about public transport in New York or a Spanish prime minister about planning in Barcelona. But I have never heard a British minister being attacked for not leaving an issue to local government. However trivial it may be – a Tube crash or a hospital operation or a social work scandal – a minister is assumed responsible and "must act". This media pressure is intense and is the chief cause of Mr Blair's restless initiatives, fuelled in turn by the media's susceptibility to league tables and name-and-shame headlines.

An entire language has evolved to deride localism: provincial, parochial, petty, civic, tin-pot, de minimis and most recently "bog standard". During the government's brief flirtation with elected mayors, the candidate in Hartlepool presented himself as the local football mascot in a monkey suit. He won and has proved himself a competent local leader, likely to be re-elected. Yet I have never debated mayors on any BBC programme without the presenter calling them "monkey mayors".

The most potent anti-localist cliché is "postcode lottery". This is applied to any evidence of a public service in one area being worse (never better) than in another. Local councils are always "under-performing", never over-performing. The post-code lottery is set up as a national disgrace. Any variation from the norm means a "lottery", be it hospital waiting times, speeding fines, GCSE results, cannabis penalties or truancy rates. Variation is a blot on the escutcheon of the state.

It will thus be hard for a minister to stand at the dispatch box and declaim, "That is not a matter for me... It is not my business... There is nothing that must be done." The idea of boasting of pluralism or diversity is anathema. It seems to be equally hard for an Opposition to take such a view. Parliament, like the media, is institutionally centralist. It is the embodiment of hyper-interventionism. As for the BBC, I cannot imagine its reporters ever challenging a politician with, "How dare you intervene in what is a local matter?"

Which brings me to the last enemy of localism, the British people. Divergent standards are the price of localism, even though centralism has not delivered consistent ones. Divergence causes anxiety. Defying the centre on a specific matter of policy is one thing. Defying a national norm in health or education, law and order or safety, requires bold choices and judgment as to risk. It requires people to indulge in local politics as never before, combing, challenging, questioning, voting.

Most people prefer a quiet life. They are inclined to agree with de Tocqueville's analysis of French bureaucracy, that it "imparts without difficulty an admirable regularity to the routine of business; provides skilfully for the details of social control... and perpetuates a drowsy regularity in the conduct of affairs." Many are comforted that ministers and civil servants are striving to protect them from what political scientists now call "the stress of choice". They have come to expect their schools, hospitals and police to be like road signs and motorway cafes, all the same. If public services are mediocre as a result, at least it is not their fault. Central government can be blamed.

British people are as ready as any other to involve themselves in voluntary and charitable activity. They join Women's Institutes, Rotary, sports clubs and help raise money for charities. They go on fun runs and organise car boots sales and gala dinners. They will even take up politics, ferociously, when threatened with an unwelcome planning application or an uncomfortable neighbourhood. They will fight hunting, and fight a hunting ban. They are like citizens anywhere if roused.

What they will not do is vote. Their politics they delegate upwards, and with a sigh of relief. It is said that a Continental European votes for someone with power over his or her life on average once a year. A Briton votes just 15 times in a lifetime, at general elections. This waning of political engagement is a retreat from commitment. It engenders that enemy of democracy, apathy.

# Conclusion

Alexis de Tocqueville is the favourite quote factory for localists. His age is not ours and his assumptions are often different. But no one better described the outcome of centralist regimes, shorn of intermediate institutions and associations. "I see each citizen standing apart, like a stranger to the destiny of others; his children and personal friends forming for him the entire human race. As for the remainder of his fellow citizens, he is beside them but he does not see them... and above them rises an immense and tutelary power", that of the state. That state would always have a vested interest in making "general indifference a sort of public virtue". He would always tend towards dictatorship.

Britain today demonstrates all de Tocqueville's fears. Britons are less democratic in their politics and less satisfied with what democracy gives them than any comparable nation. But does this matter? Most people are reasonably safe and reasonably rich. They may be badly governed. They may regard their public services as below par. But for all this they are excused too much worry, too much voting and too much caring about their fellow men and women. As we saw in the last chapter, they are relieved of a deal of hard work. Should we not just relax?

The answer is that people do not seem happy at all. The last full survey of democracy in Britain reached a grim conclusion. Only 12 per cent thought the nation was becoming more democratic. Almost 40 per cent thought the opposite.[61] Local election turnouts are now down to half the European average. Political participation is plummeting. And this is having an effect. Despite massive rises in public service spending on health and education, the public sees these services as failing. Whitehall intervention has not achieved its desired goal, a standardised and equitable pattern of welfare. The post-code lottery is rife. Targetry has not benefited the archers, only the target makers.

Nor is it true that Britain has altogether relaxed. Precisely the pressure that drove decentralisation across much of Europe, the need to avert separatism, was experienced in Britain. The response was devolution. This was against the strident opposition of the Conservative party and might never have happened had it not been implemented immediately on Labour taking office in 1997. Yet the political result was instant, a collapse in separatist sentiment and a falling off in support for Scots and Welsh nationalism. British politics, in other words, does respond when seriously challenged.

Over-centralised power never survives. It brought down the Roman, the Spanish, the Ottoman and the Austro-Hungarian empires. It reduced to brutalism the "democratic centralism" of the Soviet Union. Alex Nove's study of Lenin's 5-year-plan offers a dismal echo of Whitehall's present predicament: "A book could be filled with the list of the various expedients to encourage enterprises to act in the manner the planners wished – and the trouble to which each of them gave rise."[62] The same bureaucratic obsession is now undermining public confidence in the European Union, and appears beyond the ability of politicians to cure. The disease seems endemic to size.

The two most effective hegemonies, those created by Britain in the 19th century and the early USA, were both rooted in the Anglo-Saxon tradition of local autonomy. They are exceptions that prove the rule. From the Raj in India to the arms-length devolution of Lugard and Milner in Africa, the British Empire was a confederation of semi-autonomous governments. They owed allegiance to the Queen but were mostly ruled through local leaders. The American federalists, long predating Lugard, likewise sought a balance between the centre and "states' rights". Guarding that equilibrium has been the genius of American politics ever since. Trying to export it is now a great risk.

Modern British government has an imperialist imprint, except that it ignores the Empire's message, that it worked worst when accompanied by colonial occupation. Historians have even described British local government as that of an "internal colony".[63] When something is amiss, the response is not to devolve accountability but to centralise it. Even today the British government is moving its troops into hitherto uncharted territory, into detailed land-use planning, predict-and-provide housing, classroom administration and neighbourhood policing. A new structure of regions is asserting central control in every locality. Historic units of geographical identity are being broken up. The targets issuing each day from the Cabinet Office Delivery Unit would make even Lenin blush.

This cannot be right or sensible. As the number of elected councillors shrinks to 22,000, it is replaced by 60,000 unelected appointees of the centre, out of touch with the country and those they purport to serve. Politicians of all parties claim to recognise the evils of this and parrot the new localism. They do so even as they construct new mechanisms of control. They display the classic symptoms of Orwell's double-think, "the power of holding two contradictory beliefs in one's mind simultaneously and accepting both of them".

In 1998 the Norwegian parliament, the Storting, celebrated the millennium by appointing a commission of five wise men and women. The remit was to inquire into the democratic health of Norway a century after independence. Here was one of the most stable and prosperous countries in Europe. Election turnouts were high, politics active and people apparently content. Yet how were things really doing? Was Norwegian democracy in good enough shape to last another century?

The answer came in 50 volumes, and was stark. The commission found Norway was "a democratic infrastructure in collapse".[64] Formal participation in government was falling. Political activity was shifting from party commitment to a transient attachment to "here-and-now" groups. Norway's favoured forum of democracy, the municipality, was being railroaded by the state. The media raised public expectations but left local government with too little backing to deliver. Government, increasingly concentrated in Oslo, was falling into the hands of a network of unelected technocrats, lawyers and journalists. Though outside the European Union, Norway was finding itself trammelled by the need to accept European laws and regulations, over which it had no control at all.

In his *TLS* review of the report, Stein Ringen pointed out that even a country of great social cohesion found that "the democratic chain of command from voter to service provider was breaking". Was it conceivable, he asked, that democracy itself was becoming obsolete? Might it be as outdated as British central government now regards local?

The prescription demanded by Norway's wise men was urgent. Democratic institutions had to be reconditioned and revived. Proportional representation – not a British problem – had yielded an unresponsive national politics. More important, the once (and still) vigorous municipal democracy had to be strengthened. Pluralism needed active support. Oligarchy was not good government. Bureaucratic centralism needed new checks and balances.

Norway, in other words, was sharing the experience of all Europe in the 1980s and 1990s, and was seeking to do something about them. The experience is also Britain's. Yet from the prescription Britain stands aloof. When in 2003 it conducted a review of local government finance, it looked abroad – and with apparent approval. The government's Balance of Funding Review reported "clear parallels" between British experience and abroad and remarked on the widespread move away from centralism "towards tolerance of a greater degree of local variation in services." It added that these variations, the central objection to local democracy in Britain, "seem not to have provoked any major concerns or opposition."[65] Yet the report was shelved by ministers.

Governments that treat apathy as consent and leave democratic institutions to rot may enjoy a quiet life for a time. But they invite deteriorating public services, civil disobedience and possible separatism. They invite public cynicism which eventually withdraws consent from politics altogether. The casual manner in which Whitehall and Westminster have already acceded to the higher centralism of Brussels has removed large areas of public administration from the realm of accountable government. Apathy and cynicism seem to be spinning in a vicious circle away from traditional democratic liberties.

I believe that localism is both a refresher course in public participation and the modern way of supplying public services. It is part of a wider philosophical tradition of personal and communal responsibility to which Hume, Locke, Stuart Mill and others have long drawn attention. To deny mature citizens control over their immediate environment denies them the modern human right to self-determination. The implication rife in British politics that such self-government must be incompetent is an insult to democracy. It mocks all claims to "civic society". It derides the concern for the public realm with which the present government came to power.

British governments are constitutionally plenipotentiary. They can do what they like. They are free to join the rest of the free world and return powers and obligations to local people. Nothing stops them but their own arrogance and prejudice. They should go for localism, and with a bang.

# Notes

1 *Democracy Under Blair*, p247
2 MORI for Audit Commission, 2001
3 Commission for Local Democracy, 1995
4 Hunt, *Building Jerusalem*, p344
5 *Democracy Under Blair*, p211
6 Council of Europe and other sources, 1998–2000
7 *Democracy Under Blair, op..cit*
8 Corry and Stoker, *New Localism*, NLGN
9 Lecture, Vienna, 9.12.03
10 *Total Politics*, Conservative Political Centre, p2
11 Hunt, *op. cit*, p224
12 Olivier Borraz, *Local Leadership and Decision Marking*, Rowntree
13 Jean-Benoi Nardeau and Julie Barlow, *60m Frenchmen can't be wrong*
14 H.Mendras and A.Cole, *Social Change in Modern France*, Cambridge
15 Udo Bullmann and Edward Page, in Rowntree, *op cit*
16 *The New Centralism*, Marquand ed
17 Loughlin and Martin, *Balance of Funding Papers*, Cardiff, 2003
18 Agne Gustafsson, *Local Government in Sweden*, Stockholm, 1988
19 Elias Mossialos, Ashgate, 1999
20 Linda Weiss, in Marquand ed
21 Delcamp and Loughlin, *Balance of Funding Paper, op.cit.*
22 Putnam, *Making Democracy Work*
23 Jenkins, *Accountable to None*, Penguin
24 *Ibid.* p48
25 Travers, Tony in Marquand ed, *op. cit*
26 *Balance of Funding Papers, op. cit*
27 Jenkins, *op. cit*, p158
28 Jerry White, *Fear of Voting*, 1994
29 Nigel Lawson, *The View from No 11*, 1992
30 Power, 1994
31 *Public Finance*, 4.9.03
32 Dan Corry, ippr
33 '*New Localism, New Finance*', NLGN
34 *Public Finance*, 29.10.99
35 *Daily Telegraph*, 12.12.03
36 Reported in *Financial Times* 2.9.03
37 YouGov, TES 26.09.03
38 *Hansard*, 17.3.02
39 *The Times*, 28.02.04
40 *The Times*, 14.08.04
41 Audit Commission, annual returns
42 Jenkins, *op. cit.*, p105
43 *Public Finance*, 5.12.03
44 *Guardian*, 21.07.04
45 NLGN, 2004
46 *Guardian*, 2.8.04
47 *British Medical Journal*, June 04
48 *The Times*,31.8.04
49 *Public Finance*, 28.11.02
50 Paddy Ashdown, *Diaries*, 2001
51 B.Hogwood, *Mapping the Regions*, 1996
52 Loughlin and Martin, *Balance of Funding Papers, op. cit*
53 *New Localism, New Finance*, NLGN
54 Policy Exchange and New Economics Foundation, September 2004
55 *Making Sense of Localism*, John Smith Institute
56 *Vexed and Troubled Englishmen*
57 *The British Constitution Now*, 1992
58 Hugo Young and Anne Sloman, BBC, 1984
59 Lawson, *op. cit*
60 Hunt, *op. cit*, p.225
61 Commission for Local Democracy, p13
62 *Economic History of the USSR*
63 John Davies, *History of Wales*, p225
64 'The Norwegian Study of Power and Democracy', see *TLS* review, 13.2.04
65 Loughlin and Martin, Balance of Funding Papers, *op. cit*

# Index

# Bibliography


Barnes, John et al, *Federal Britain*, 1998, Centre for Policty Studies

Batley, Richard and Gerry Stoker *Local Government in Europe*, 1991

Borraz, Olivier et al, *Local Leadership and Decision Making*, 1994, Joseph Rowntree

Butler, David et al, *Failure in British Government*, 1994, OUP

Clark, Greg and James Mather, *Total Politics*, 2003, Conservative Political Centre

Coles, Jo ed, *Making Sense of Localism*, 2004, Adam Smith Institute

Commission for Local Democracy, *Taking Charge: The Rebirth of Local Democracy*, 1995, Municipal Journal

Corry, Dan ed, *London Calling*, 2004, NLGN

Corry, Dan ed, *Joining-up Local Democracy*, 2004, NLGN

Corry, Dan and Gerry Stoker, *New Localism*, 2003, NLGN

Corry, Dan and Gerry Stoker, *Towards a New Localism- Re-fashioning the centre local relationship*, 2001 NLGN

Crouch, Colin and David Marquand, *The New Centralism*, 1989, Blackwell

*Democracy Under Blair*, David Beetham et al, 2002, University of Essex/Politico's

Gray, Clive, *Government beyond the Centre*, 1994, Macmillan

Green, David and Benedict Irvine, *Health Care in France and Germany*, 2001, Civitas

Gustafsson, Agne, *Local Government in Sweden*, 1998, The Swedish Institute, Stockholm

Jenkins, Simon, *Accountable to None, the Tory Nationalisation of Britain*, 1995, Penguin

John, Peter, *Local Governance in Western Europe*, 2001, Sage

Jowell, Jeffrey and Dawn Oliver, *The Changing Constitution*, 1994, Clarendon

Klein, Rudolph, *The Politics of the National Health Service*, 1989, Longman

Lawson, Nigel, *The View from No 11*, 1992 Bantam

Loughlin, John and Steve Martin, *Local Income Tax in Sweden*, Feb 2004, Balance of Funding Review, ODPM/Cardiff

Loveday, Barry and Anna Reid, *Going Local-who should run Britain's Police?*, 2003, Policy Exchange

Marquand, David, *Decline of the Public*, 2004, Polity/Blackwell

Morris, Robert ed, *Central and Local Control of Education*, 1990, Longman

Nardeau, Jean-Benoi and Julie Barlow, *60m Frenchmen can't be Wrong*, 2004

O'Neill, Martin ed, *Devolution and British Politics*, 2004, Pearson/Longman

Power, Michael, *The Audit Explosion*, 1994, Demos

Prochaskam, Frank, *Schools of Citizenship*, 2004, Civitas

Putnam, Robert, *Making Democracy Work*, 1993 Princetown University Press

Putnam, Robert, *Bowling Alone*, Simon and Schuster

Randle, Anna, *Mayors Mid-term*, 2004, NLGN

Reid M.P., Rt Hon John, *Localising the NHS*, 2003, NLGN/New Health Network

Reiner, Robert, *The Politics of the Police*, 1992, Wheatsheef

Stewart, John and Gerry Stoker, *The Future of Local Government*, 1989, Macmillan

Stoker, Gerry, *The Politics of Local Government*, 1991, Macmillan

Stoker, Gerry, *Transforming Local Governance, From Thatcher to New Labour*, 2003, Palgrave Macmillan

Thatcher, Margaret, *The Downing Street Years*, 1993, HarperCollins

Travers, Tony and Lorena Esposito, *I'm a Local Councillor, Get Me Out of Here!*, 2004, Policy Exchange

Young, Hugo and Anne Sloman, *But Chancellor*, 1984, BBC